Igor Sukhin

Chess Camp

Volume 1: Move, Attack, and Capture

MONGOOSE
Press

Publisher: Mongoose Press
1005 Boylston Street, Suite 324
Newton Highlands, MA 02461
info@mongoosepress.com
www.MongoosePress.com
ISBN: 9781936277070
Library of Congress Control Number: 2010932524
Distributed to the trade by National Book Network
custserv@nbnbooks.com, 800-462-6420
For all other sales inquiries please contact the publisher.
Printed in the United States of America

Editor: Jorge Amador
Typesetting: Frisco Del Rosario
Cover Design: Al Dianov
First English edition
0 987654321

Contents

Note for Coaches, Parents, Teachers, and Trainers

This collection of problems opens a series of a new kind of problem books. Some of the problems in it may seem absurdly simple to experienced chessplayers or coaches. But that isn't the case – the simplicity of our problems is superficial. If the required attention hasn't been paid in the past to the development of these kinds of simple problems, that highlights the fact that there are still many blank spots in the matter of how to begin teaching the game of chess. This has to do with the fact that, in every country in the world, these problem books are written by strong practical players, for whom certain subjects seem too simple to be worth any attention at all. Such authors don't take into account the fact that the earliest stage of instruction deserves closer attention.

As a result, in previously published problem collections, a large stratum of useful chess exercises has remained unrevealed. The main goal of our series of problem books is to correct this omission.

In order for the beginning chessplayer to learn to play chess well later on, the coach should first help him or her to establish a solid foundation. To this end, beginning players should first get the feel of the possibilities of each piece separately, and also familiarize themselves with the comparative strengths of the pieces. Our series of thematic exercises with a small number of pieces on the board serves this purpose.

Problem books are written by strong practical players for whom certain subjects seem too simple, leaving many useful chess exercises unrevealed...

At the same time problems from the so-called "pre-checkmate" period play a very important role in the initial stage of instruction. Very often there aren't even kings in these diagrams, such that in order to win you simply have to eliminate or immobilize all your opponent's pawns or pieces (as in checkers – play for a wipeout).

The point of these exercises isn't to deliver mate, but to acquire various chess skills, to master the simplest methods of attacking and defending. The purpose is to teach the student to see the chess board, to find hidden threats and connections between different pieces, and to understand how to coordinate the pieces to achieve one goal or another.

By using our problem book, in the course of initial study beginning chessplayers can: 1) familiarize themselves with the possibilities and comparative strengths of each piece; 2) learn to attack one piece with another piece; 3) learn how to restrict the mobility of their opponents' pieces; 4) learn to see guarded and unguarded pieces on the board; 5) learn to deliver double attacks; 6) learn to find defensive moves; 7) learn to use pins for attack and defense; 8) learn to choose the best capture from several possibilities; 9) master the typical methods of fighting with the various pieces against pawns; 10) learn to see opportunities to announce check in any position; and 11) completely master the rules of the game.

In general, in order to achieve success in chess three stages of instruction need to be covered thoroughly: 1) the "pre-checkmate" stage – here, students should develop a feel for the "pre-checkmate" harmony of the pieces in both attack and defense; 2) the stage of giving mate in one – here students should get a feel for the harmony of the pieces when checkmating; 3) the checkmate stage – here students should get a feel for the harmony of the pieces when using a mate threat. Having said that, the younger the student, the longer the first two stages should last.

This first problem book allows us to work through the first ("pre-checkmate") stage, while the second and third books focus on working through the second stage (giving mate in one). Subsequent collections will help students and coaches to work through the third (mating) stage.

The Rook

Capturing

White to move: Can White take Black's rook?

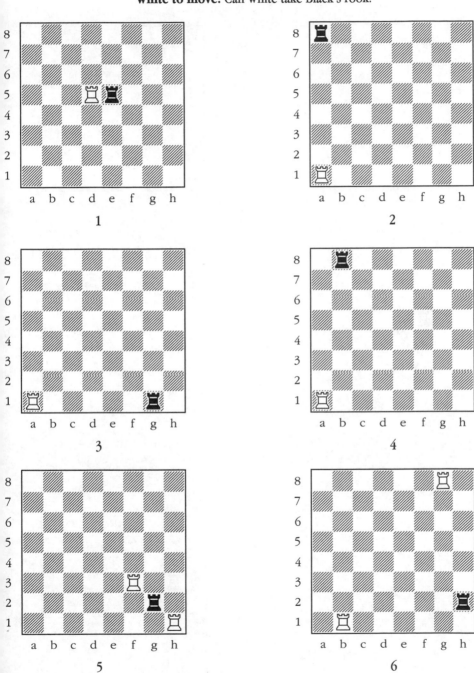

The Rook

Pieces under attack

Black to move: Take one of the white rooks.

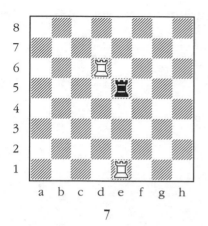

7

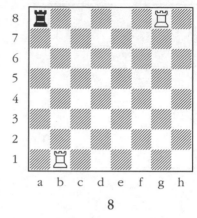

8

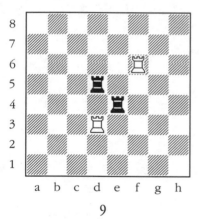

9

10

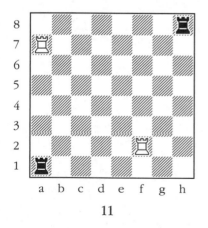

11

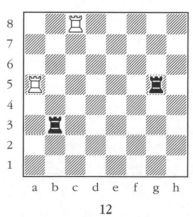

12

8

The Rook

To take or not to take?

White to move: If White captures a black rook, can Black then take the white rook?

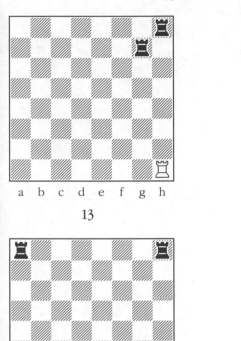

13

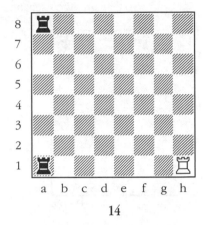

14

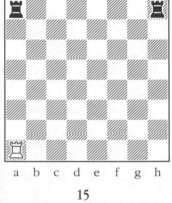

15

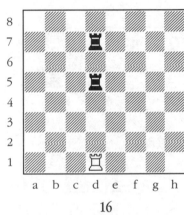

16

17

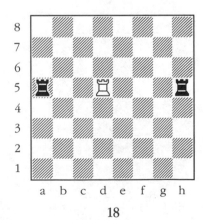

18

The Rook

The best move

Black to move: Which rook should Black take,
so that after the exchanges Black has more rooks than White?

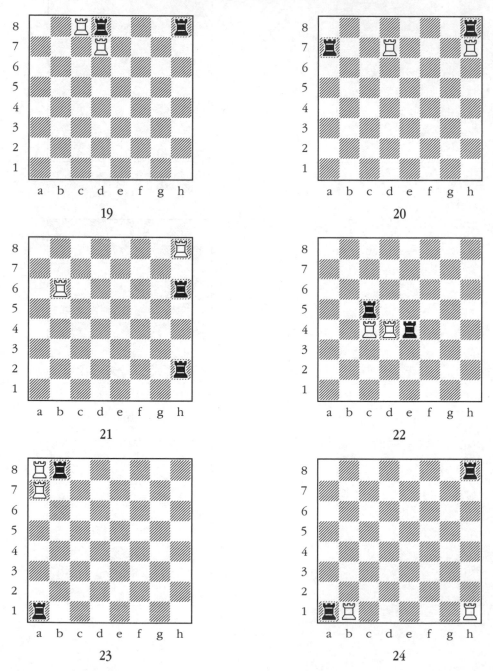

19

20

21

22

23

24

The Bishop

Capturing

White to move: Can White take the black bishop?

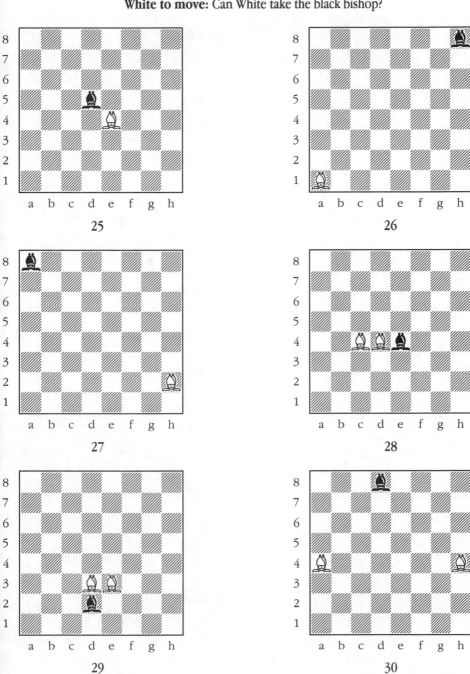

25

26

27

28

29

30

The Bishop

Under attack

Black to move: Take the white bishop.

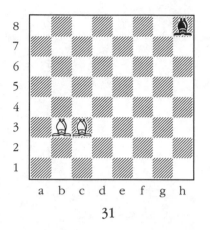

31

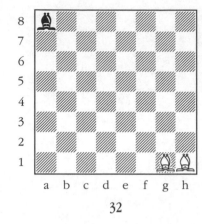

32

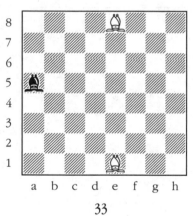

33

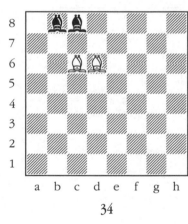

34

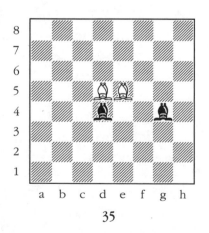

35

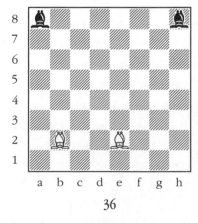

36

The Bishop
A choice

White to move: Which of the white bishops can capture?

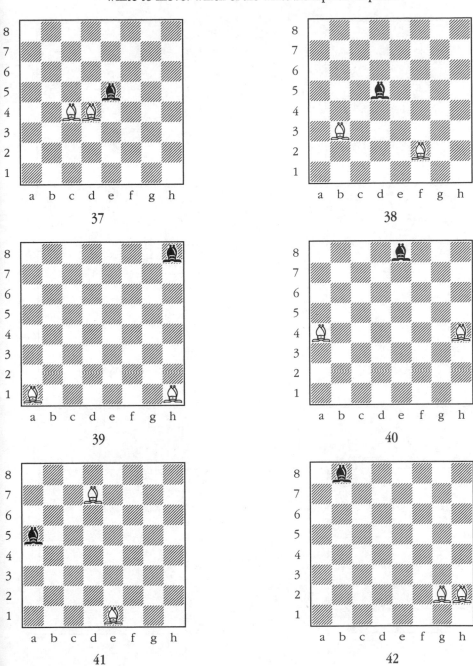

37

38

39

40

41

42

Rooks and Bishops
Attacks by the rook
White to move: Which two rook moves attack the bishop?

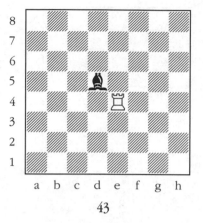

43

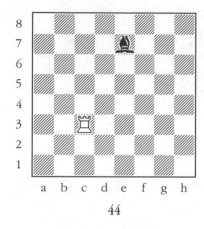

44

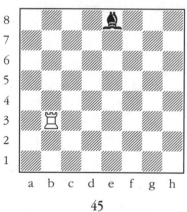

45

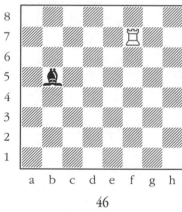

46

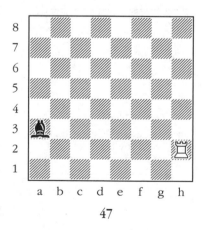

47

48

Rooks and Bishops

Bishop attacks

Black to move: Attack the rook with the bishop.

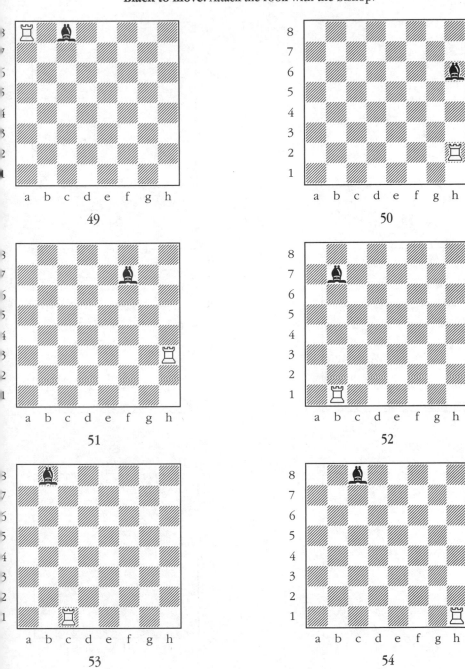

49

50

51

52

53

54

Rooks and Bishops

Double attack by the rook

White to move: Attack both bishops with the rook.

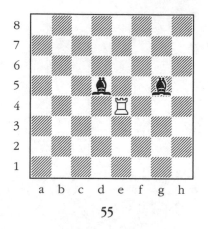

55

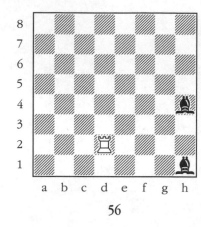

56

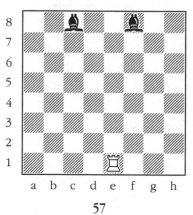

57

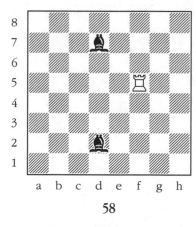

58

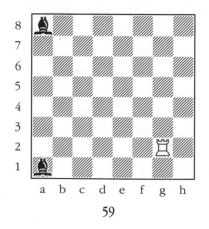

59

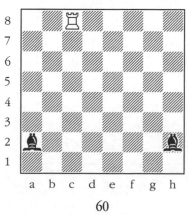

60

Rooks and Bishops

Double attack by the bishop

Black to move: Attack both rooks with the bishop.

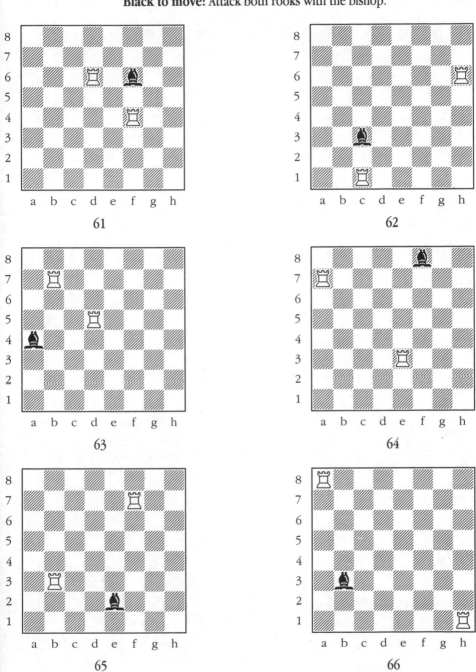

61

62

63

64

65

66

Rooks and Bishops

Skewer by the rook

White to move: Win a bishop by putting the rook on the same rank or file as the two bishops.

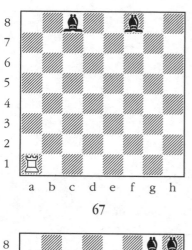

67

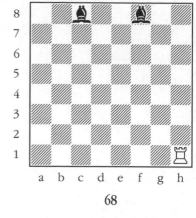

68

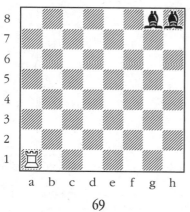

69

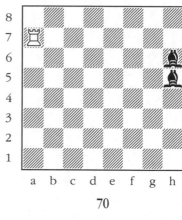

70

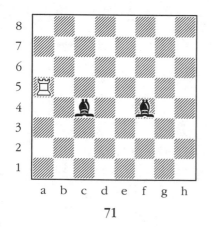

71

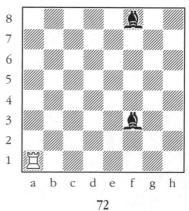

72

Rooks and Bishops

Skewer by the bishop

Black to move: Put the bishop on the same diagonal as the rooks to skewer them.

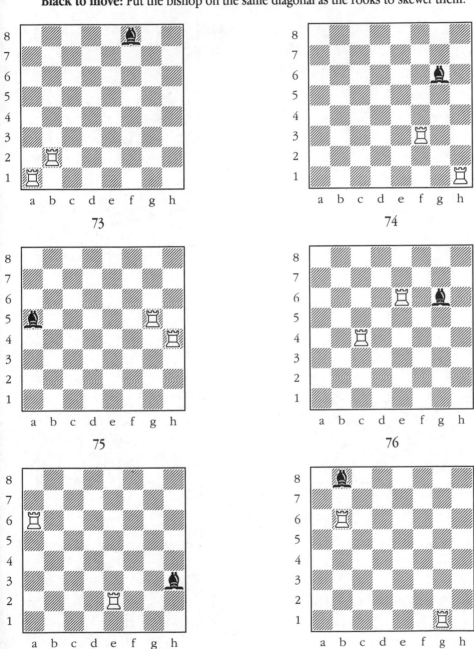

73

74

75

76

77

78

Rooks and Bishops

Capturing

White to move: Take the undefended black piece.

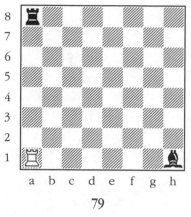

79

80

81

82

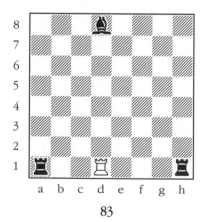

83

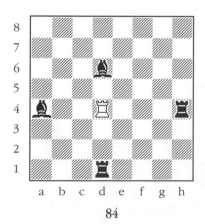

84

Rooks and Bishops

The pin

White to move: After which move by White does Black lose
either the bishop or the rook, no matter what?

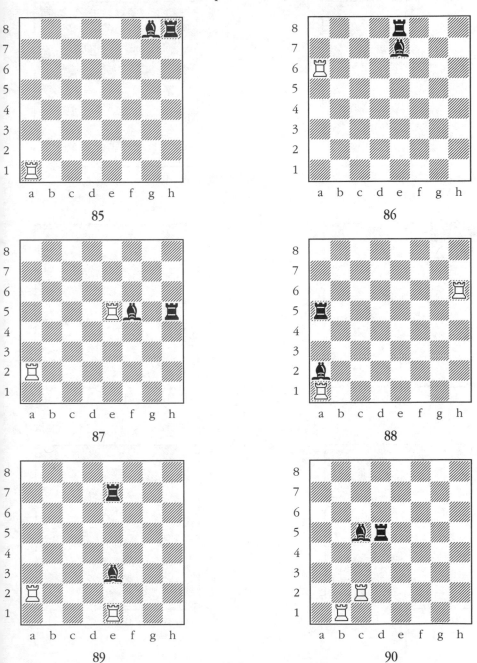

85

86

87

88

89

90

Rooks and Bishops
Escapes
Black to move: How does Black avoid losing material?

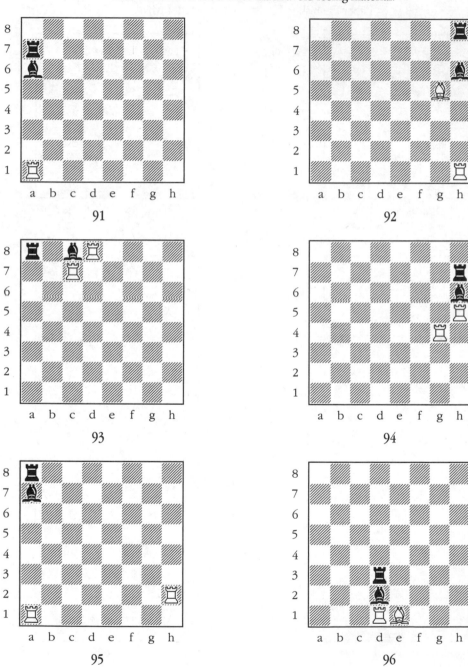

91

92

93

94

95

96

Rooks and Bishops

Defending

White to move: How does White avoid losing a piece?

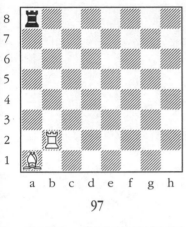

97

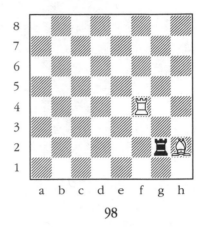

98

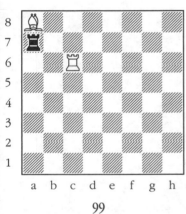

99

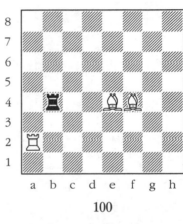

100

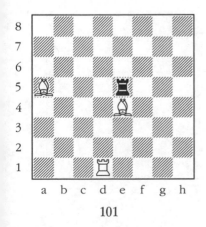

101

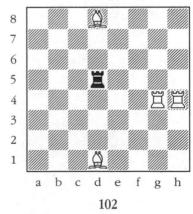

102

Rooks and Bishops

Exchanging

Black to move: Force the exchange of a white piece.

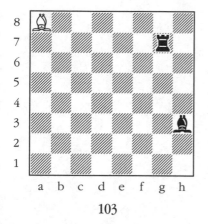

103

104

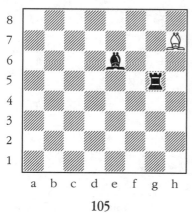

105

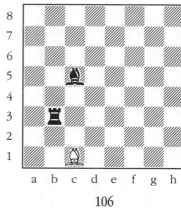

106

107

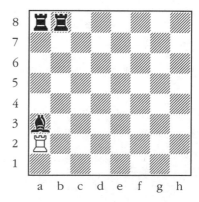

108

Rooks and Bishops

Combinations

White to move: Find the best maneuver.

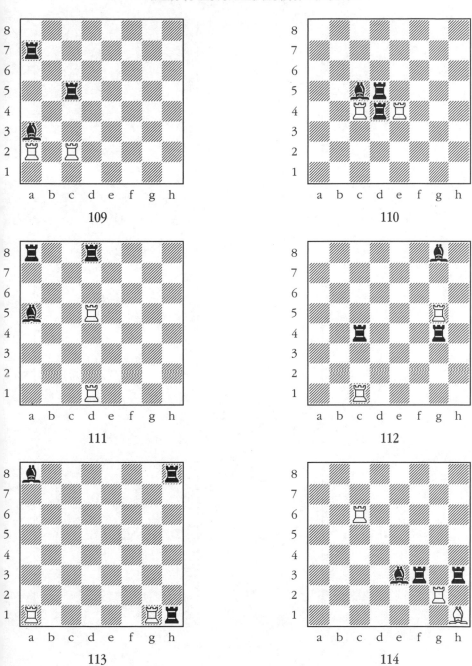

109

110

111

112

113

114

The Queen

Capturing

White to move: Can White take Black's queen?

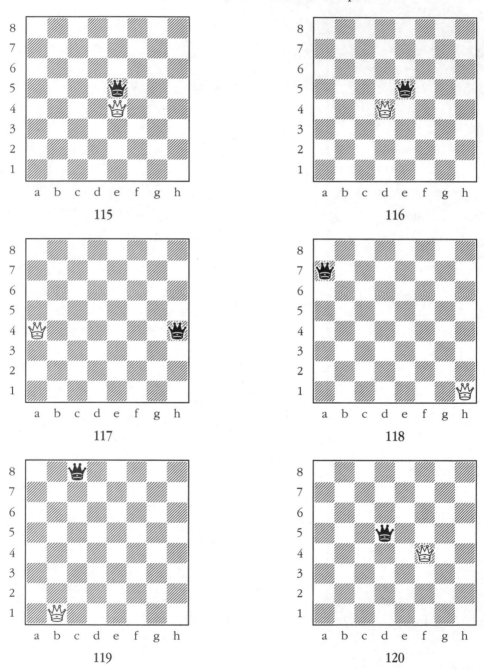

115

116

117

118

119

120

26

Queens, Rooks, and Bishops

Attack on the rook

Black to move: Without putting the queen in danger, attack the rook.

121

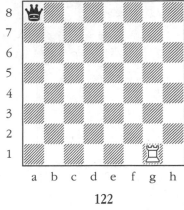

122

123

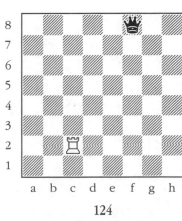

124

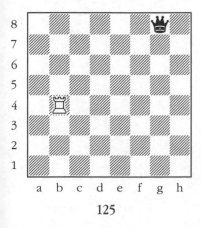

125

126

Queens, Rooks, and Bishops

Attack on the bishop

White to move: Without putting the queen in danger, find three different ways to attack the bishop.

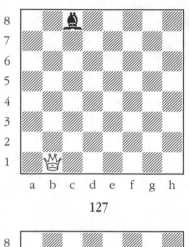

127

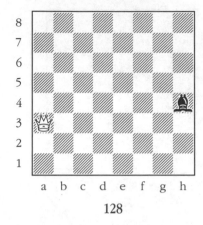

128

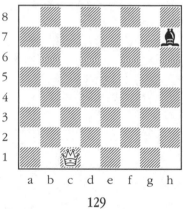

129

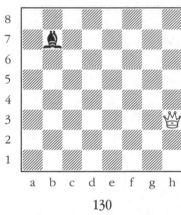

130

131

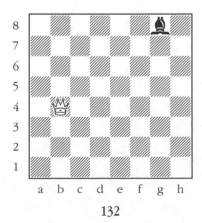

132

Queens, Rooks, and Bishops
Double attack

White to move: Without putting the queen in danger, attack both bishops at once.

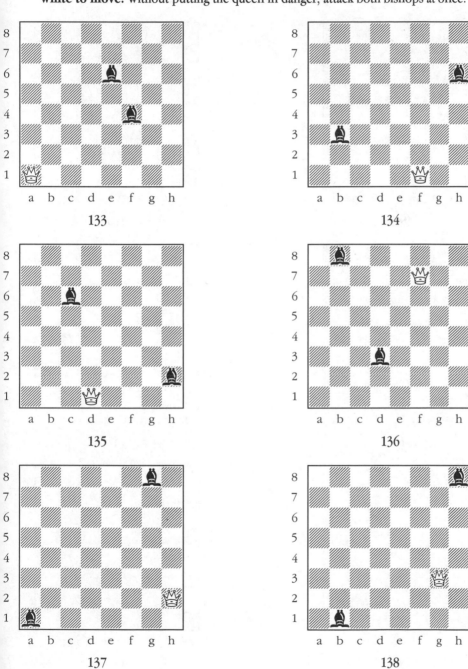

133

134

135

136

137

138

Queens, Rooks, and Bishops

Double attack

Black to move: Without putting the queen in danger, attack two pieces at once.

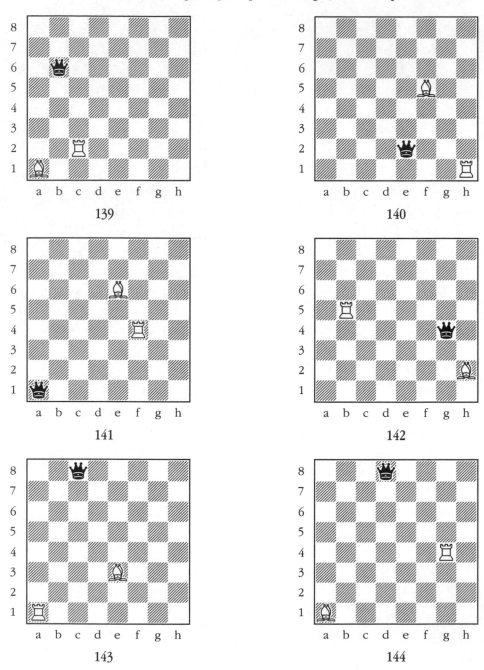

139

140

141

142

143

144

Queens, Rooks, and Bishops

Defending

White to move: How can both pieces be saved?

145

146

147

148

149

150

Queens, Rooks, and Bishops

Capturing

Black to move: Take the undefended piece.

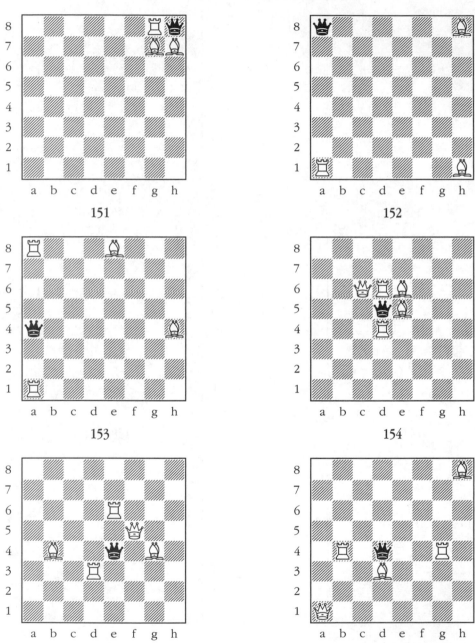

151

152

153

154

155

156

Queens, Rooks, and Bishops

The pin

White to move: Find the best chance.

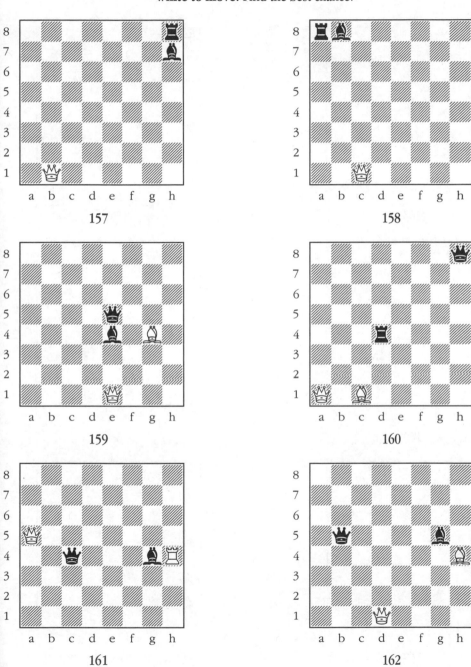

157

158

159

160

161

162

Queens, Rooks, and Bishops

Restricting mobility

Black to move: Force a trade of the white queen.

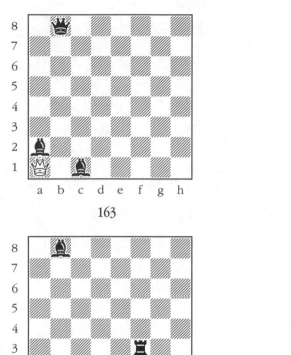

163

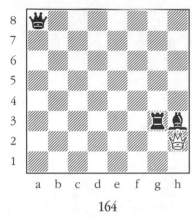

164

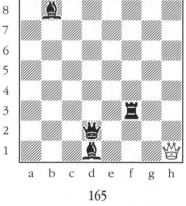

165

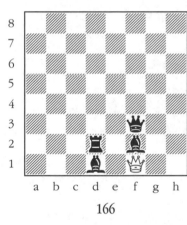

166

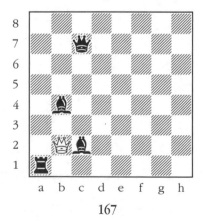

167

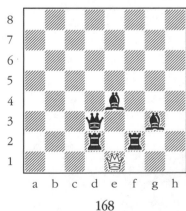

168

Queens, Rooks, and Bishops

Escapes

White to move: Find the best move.

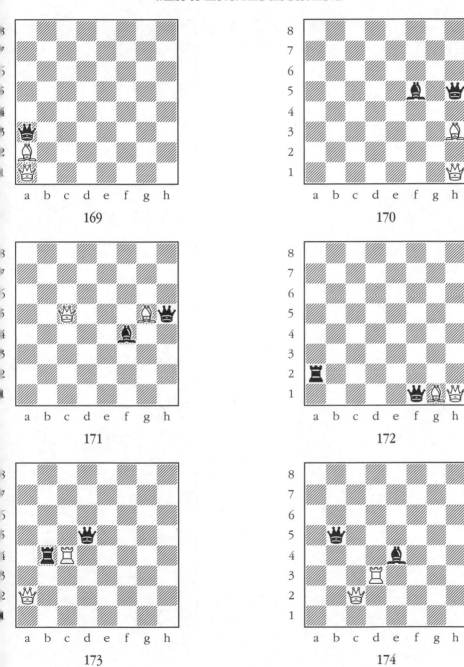

169

170

171

172

173

174

The Knight

Capturing

White to move: Can White take the black knight?

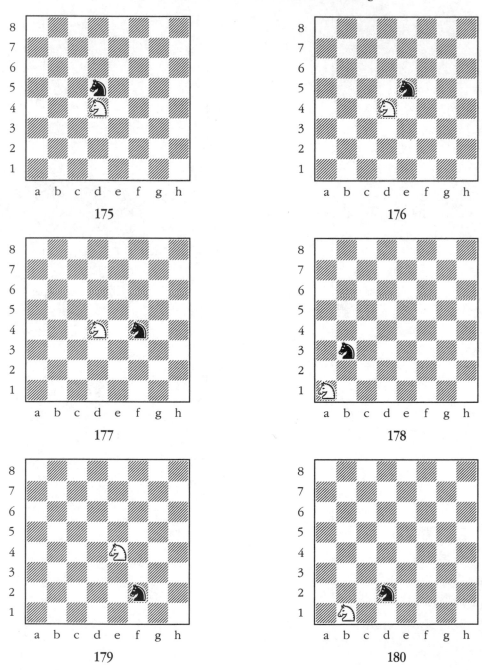

175

176

177

178

179

180

The Knight

The knight under attack

Black to move: Which knight can be taken?

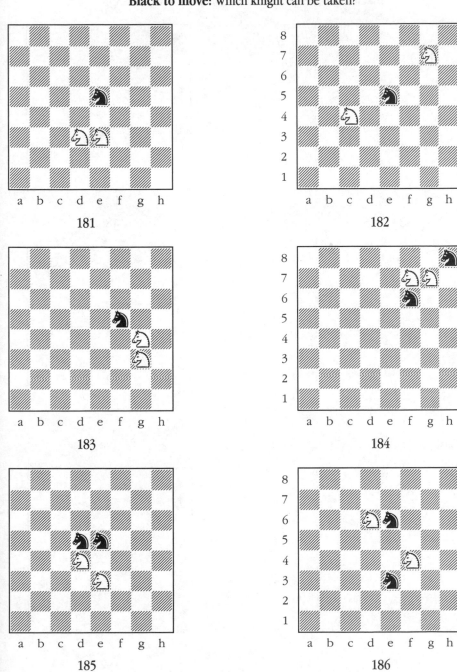

181

182

183

184

185

186

The Knight

Running past the guard

Black to move: Where should the black knight jump?

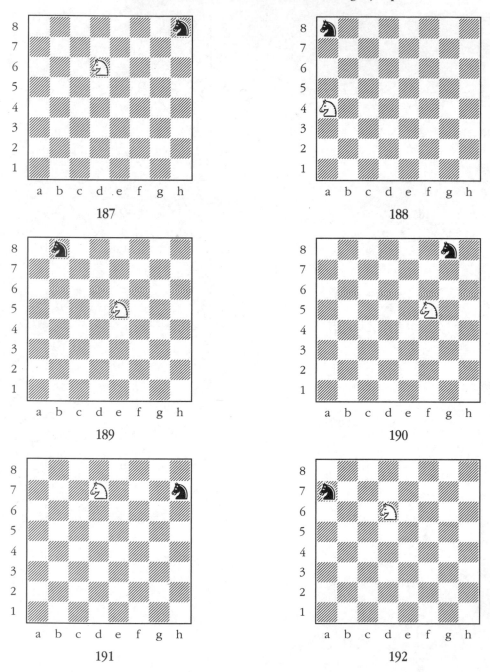

187

188

189

190

191

192

The Knight

To take or not to take?

White to move: If White captures a knight, can Black then recapture?

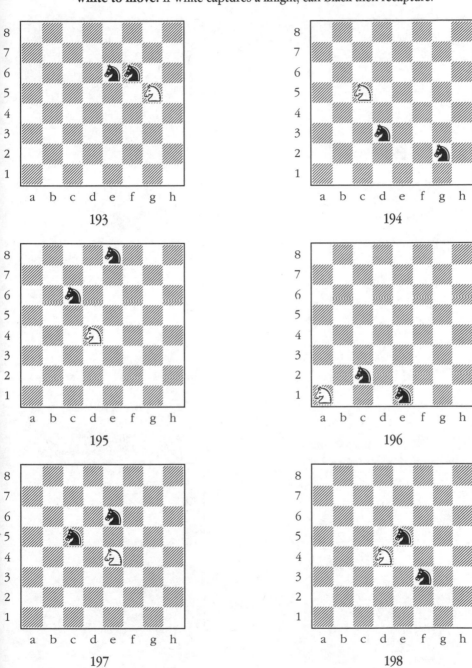

193

194

195

196

197

198

The Knight
Restricting mobility

Black to move: Which move leads to capturing the white knight?

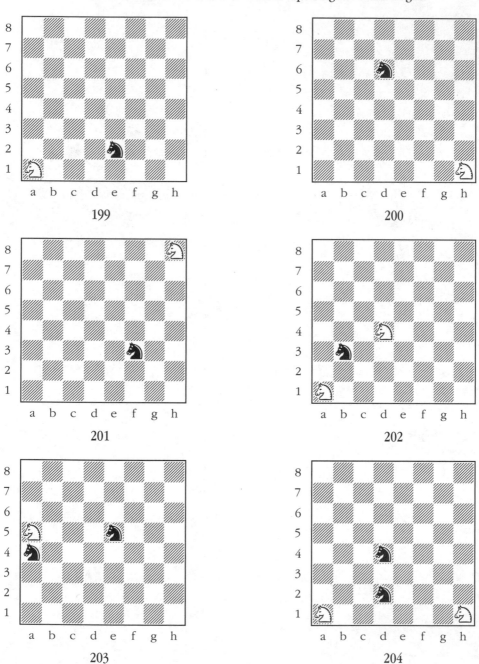

199

200

201

202

203

204

Knights, Queens, Rooks, and Bishops

The rook tames the knight

White to move: Which maneuver leads to capturing the black knight?

205

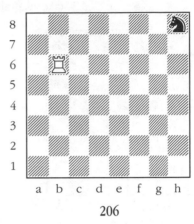

206

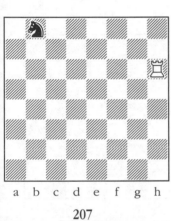

207

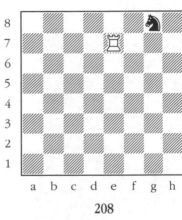

208

209

210

Knights, Queens, Rooks, and Bishops

The bishop tames the knight

White to move: Catch the black knight in a trap — in one move, take away all of its retreat squares.

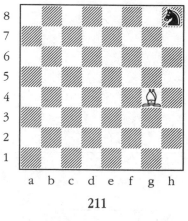

211

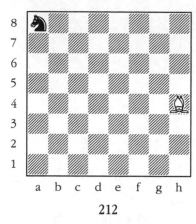

212

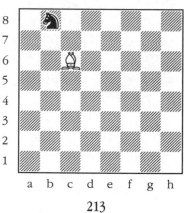

213

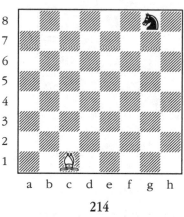

214

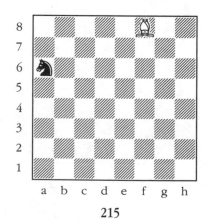

215

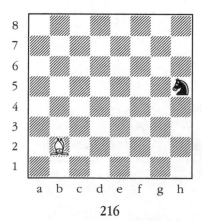

216

Knights, Queens, Rooks, and Bishops
The queen tames the knight

Black to move: Catch the white knight in a trap — in one move, take away all of its retreat squares.

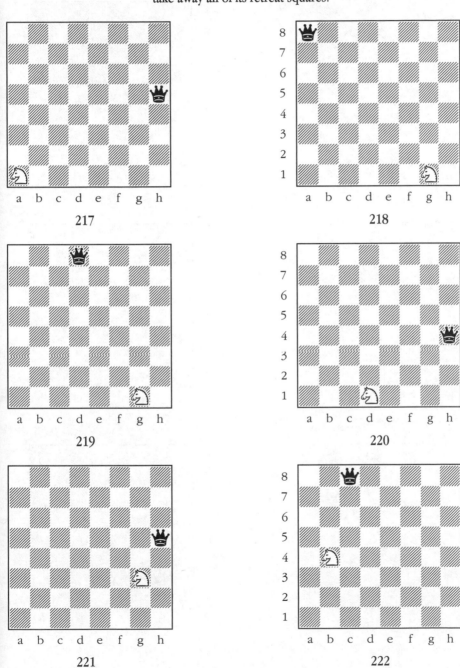

217

218

219

220

221

222

Knights, Queens, Rooks, and Bishops

Attacks by the knight

White to move: Attack an enemy piece with the knight.

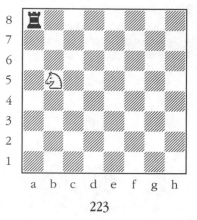

223

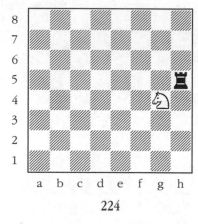

224

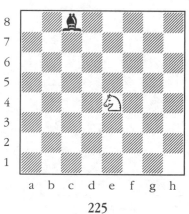

225

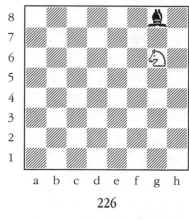

226

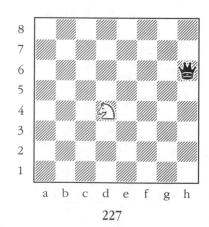

227

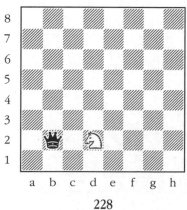

228

44

Knights, Queens, Rooks, and Bishops

Double attack

Black to move: Attack two white pieces with the black knight.

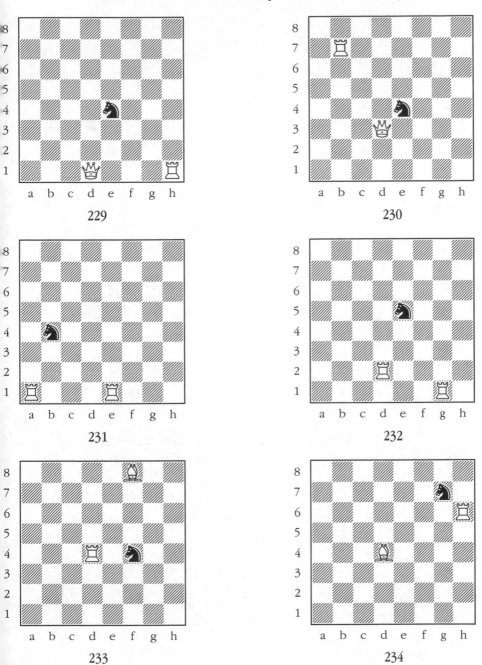

229

230

231

232

233

234

Knights, Queens, Rooks, and Bishops

Capturing an undefended piece

White to move: Take an undefended piece with the knight.

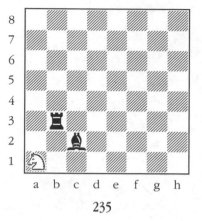

235

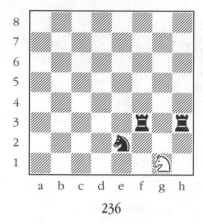

236

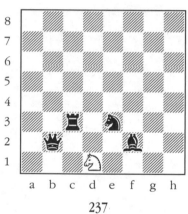

237

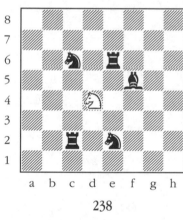

238

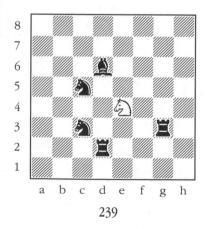

239

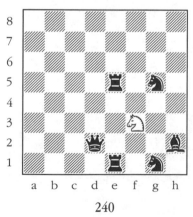

240

Knights, Queens, Rooks, and Bishops
Defending
Black to move: How to save the piece?

241

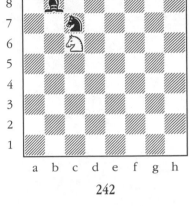

242

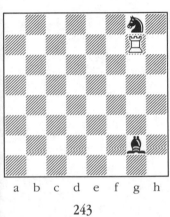

243

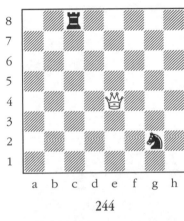

244

245

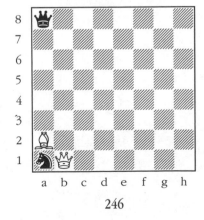

246

Knights, Queens, Rooks, and Bishops

The pin

White to move: Win a piece.

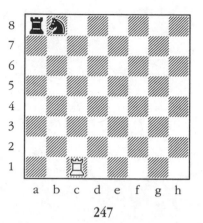

247

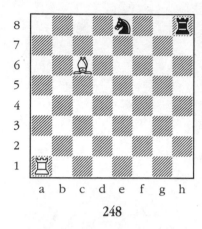

248

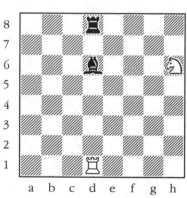

249

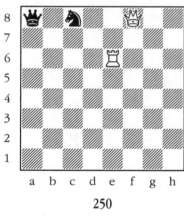

250

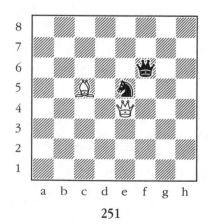

251

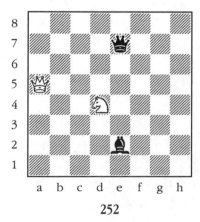

252

48

Knights, Queens, Rooks, and Bishops

Escapes

Black to move: Find the best chance.

253

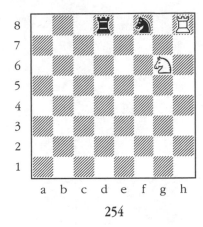

254

255

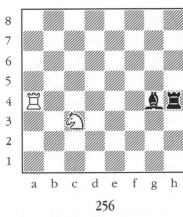

256

257

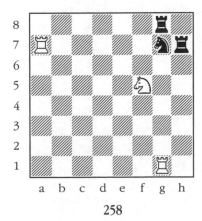

258

The Pawn

Capturing

White to move: Can the black pawn be taken?

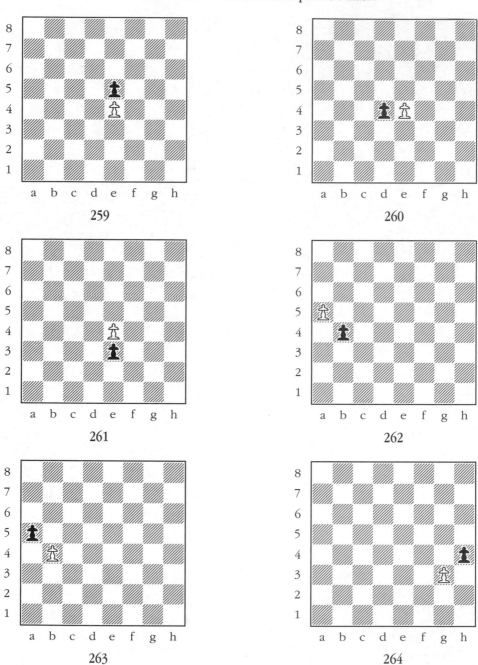

259

260

261

262

263

264

The Pawn

The only move

Black to move: There is only one possibility.

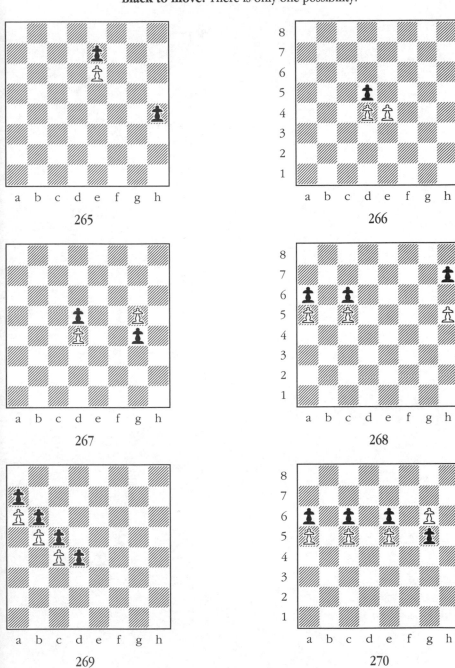

265

266

267

268

269

270

The Pawn

Captures

White to move: Which pawn can be taken?

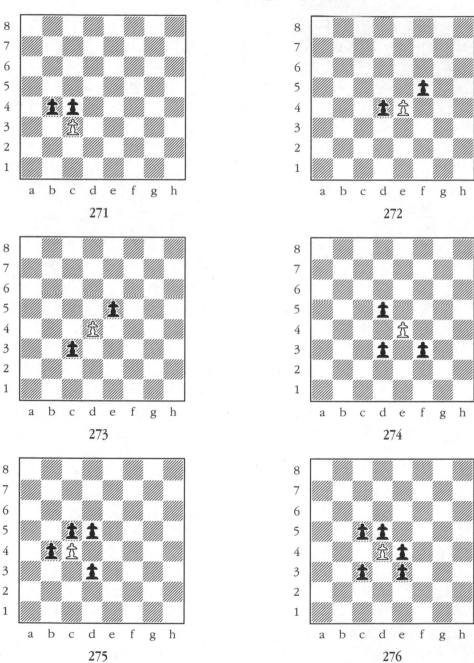

271

272

273

274

275

276

The Pawn

To take or not to take?

Black to move: Should Black take White's pawn?

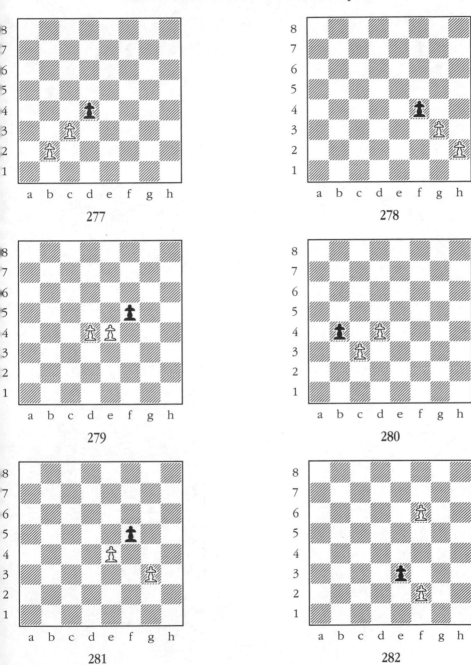

277

278

279

280

281

282

The Pawn

The best capture

White to move: Which pawn is better to take?

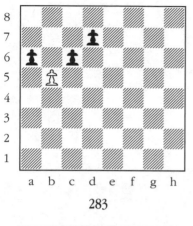

283

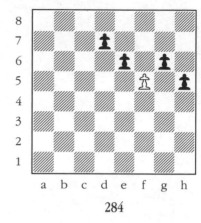

284

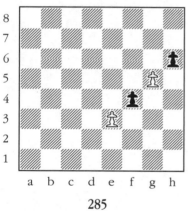

285

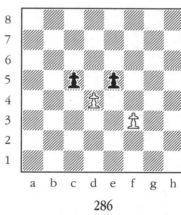

286

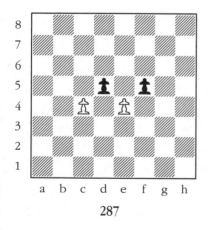

287

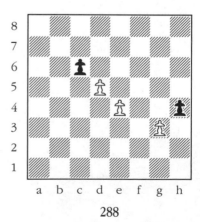

288

The Pawn

Restricting mobility

Black to move: Find the best opportunity.

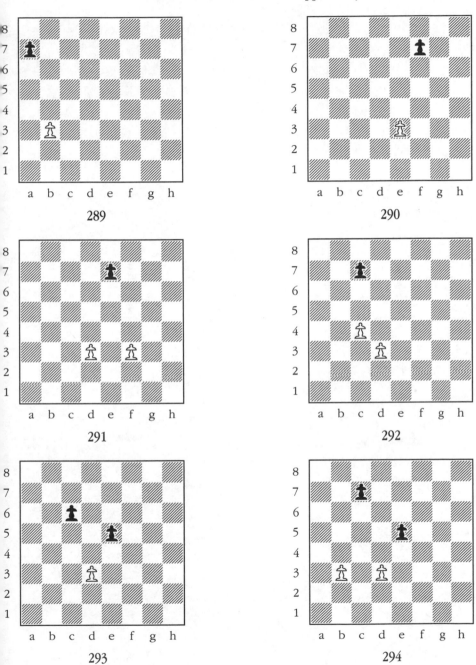

289

290

291

292

293

294

The Pawn

The blockade

White to move: Prevent Black from making a move in reply.

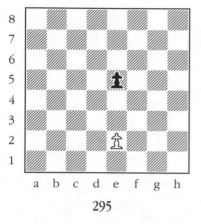

295

296

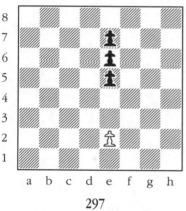

297

298

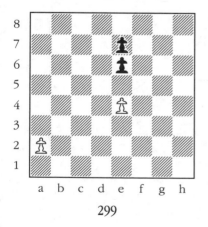

299

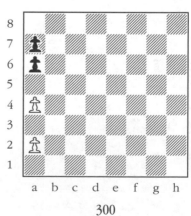

300

The Pawn

Pawn promotion

Black to move: Which piece should the black pawn be promoted to, so that the white pawn is under attack?

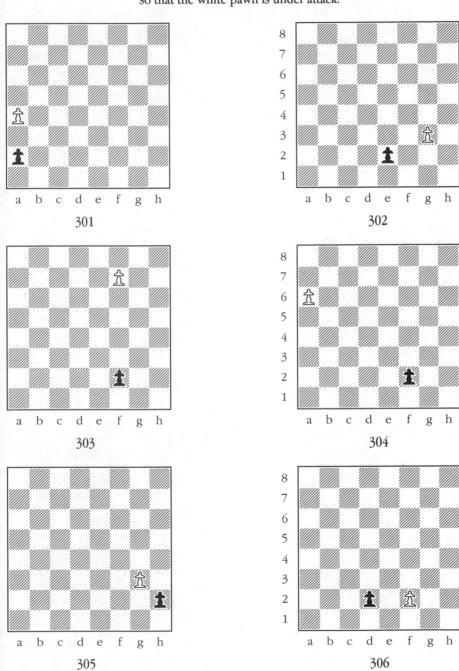

301

302

303

304

305

306

The Pawn

The breakthrough

Black to move: Which maneuver allows one of the black pawns to promote to a queen first?

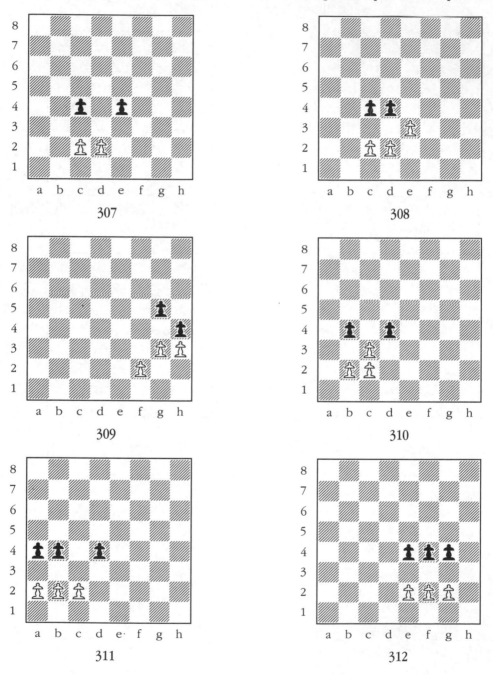

The Pawn
The breakthrough

White to move: Which maneuver allows one of the white pawns to promote to a queen first?

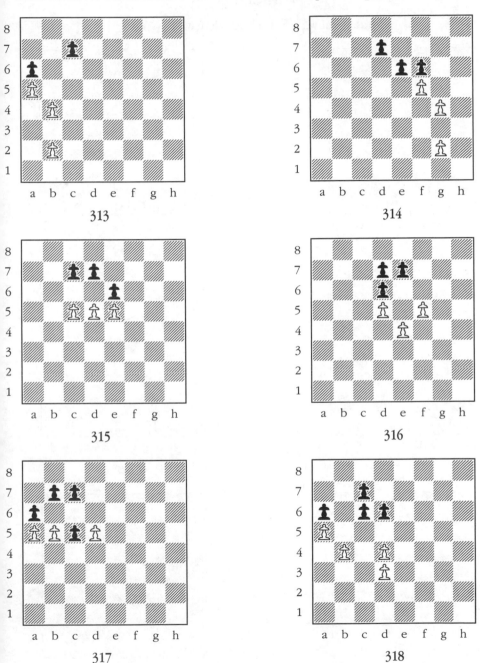

313

314

315

316

317

318

Pawns, Knights, Queens, Rooks, and Bishops

Attacking

White to move: Attack a black piece with a pawn.

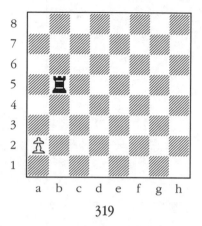

319

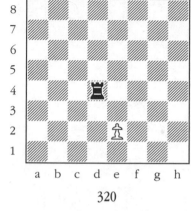

320

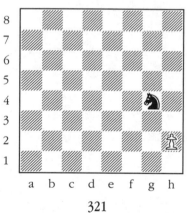

321

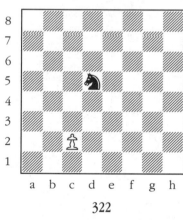

322

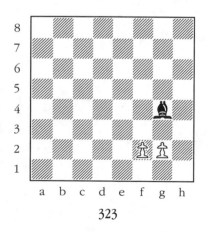

323

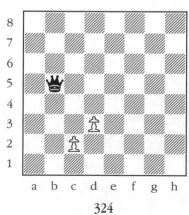

324

Pawns, Knights, Queens, Rooks, and Bishops

Double attack

Black to move: Attack two white pieces with a pawn.

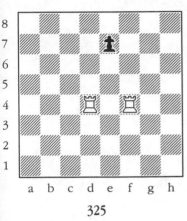

325

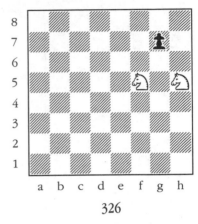

326

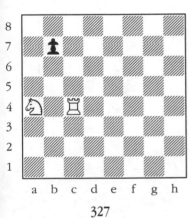

327

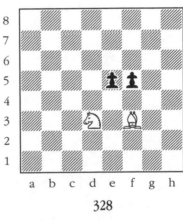

328

329

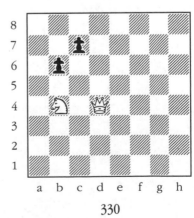

330

Pawns, Knights, Queens, Rooks, and Bishops

Capturing an undefended piece

White to move: Take an undefended piece.

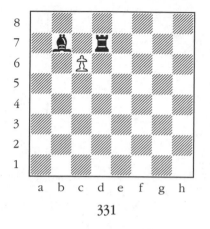

331

332

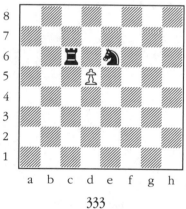

333

334

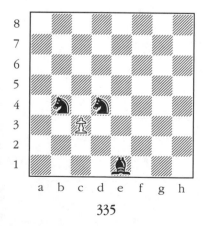

335

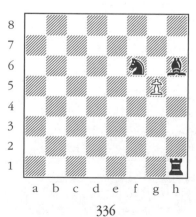

336

Pawns, Knights, Queens, Rooks, and Bishops

The pin

Black to move: Win a piece.

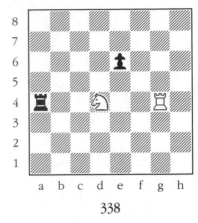

337

338

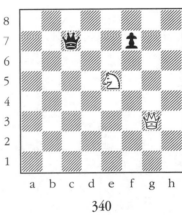

339

340

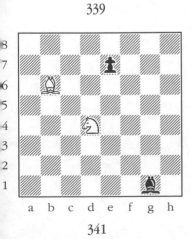

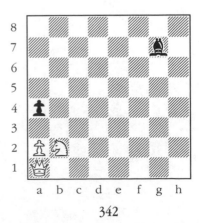

341

342

Pawns, Knights, Queens, Rooks, and Bishops
Defending

White to move: Defend a pawn or a piece that is under attack.

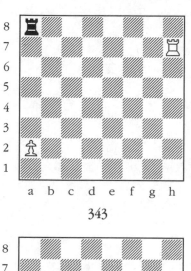

343

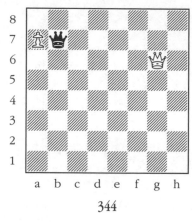

344

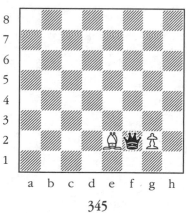

345

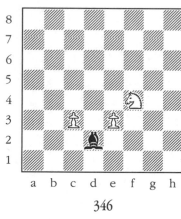

346

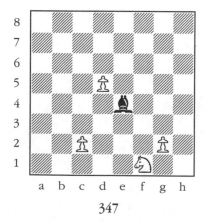

347

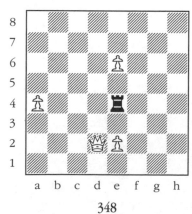

348

Pawns, Knights, Queens, Rooks, and Bishops

Escapes

Black to move: Save a pawn or a piece.

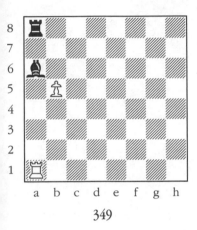

349

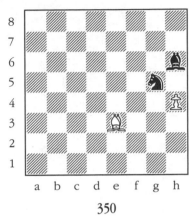

350

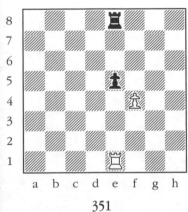

351

352

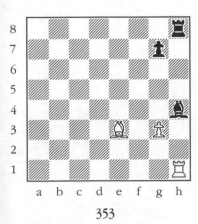

353

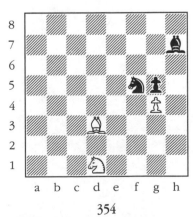

354

Pawns, Knights, Queens, Rooks, and Bishops

Restricting mobility

White to move: Stop the black pawn.

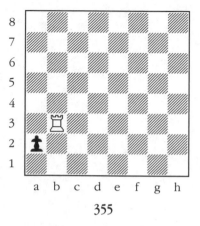

355

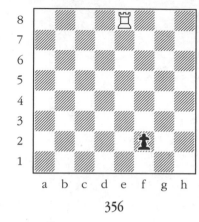

356

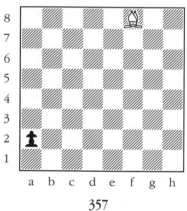

357

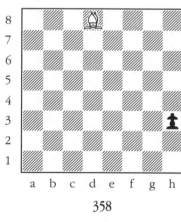

358

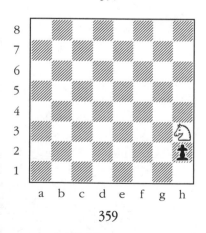

359

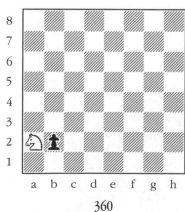

360

Pawns, Knights, Queens, Rooks, and Bishops

Rook against two pawns

White to move: Find the way to defeat the pawns.

361

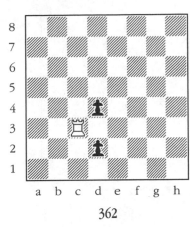

362

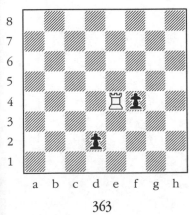

363

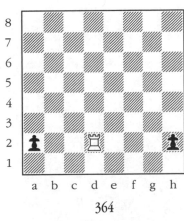

364

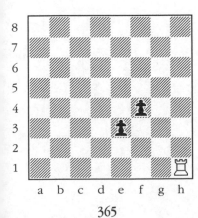

365

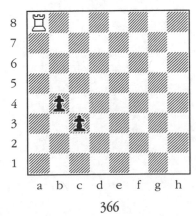

366

Pawns, Knights, Queens, Rooks, and Bishops

Two pawns against a rook

Black to move: Promote at least one of the pawns to a queen.

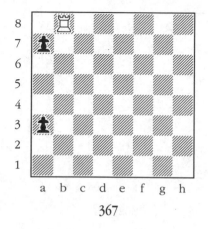

367

368

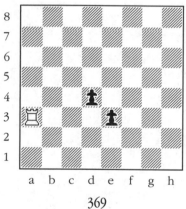

369

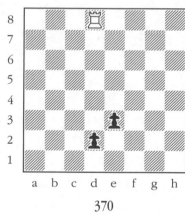

370

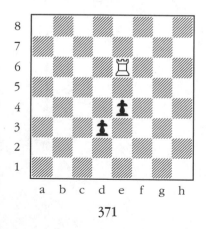

371

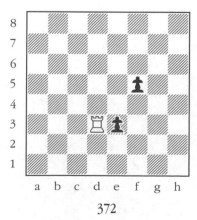

372

Pawns, Knights, Queens, Rooks, and Bishops

Bishop against two pawns

White to move: Find the path to victory.

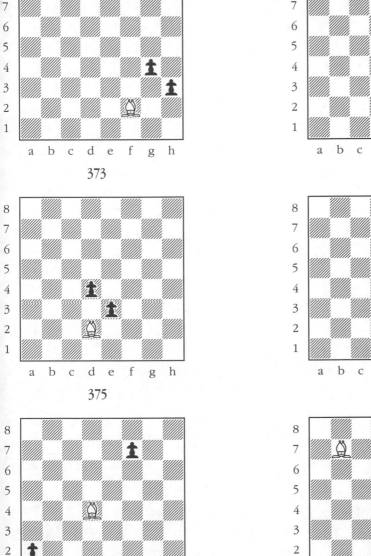

373

374

375

376

377

378

Pawns, Knights, Queens, Rooks, and Bishops

Two pawns against a bishop

Black to move: Promote at least one of the pawns to a queen.

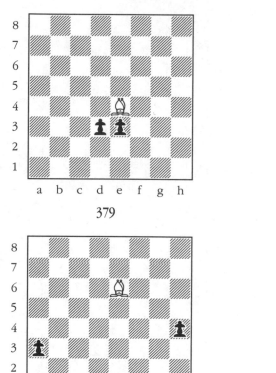

379

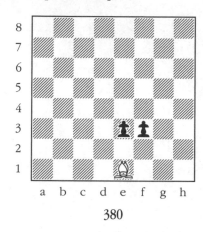

380

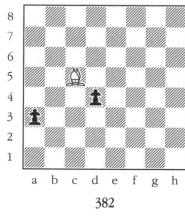

381

382

383

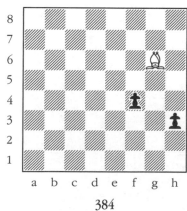

384

Pawns, Knights, Queens, Rooks, and Bishops

Knight against two pawns

White to move: Find the path to victory.

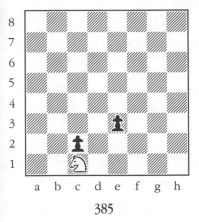

385

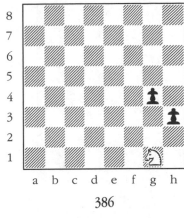

386

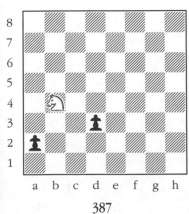

387

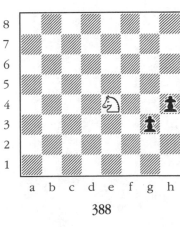

388

389

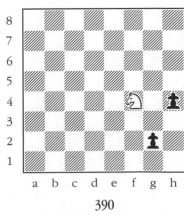

390

Pawns, Knights, Queens, Rooks, and Bishops

Two pawns against a knight

Black to move: Promote at least one of the pawns to a queen, or trap the knight.

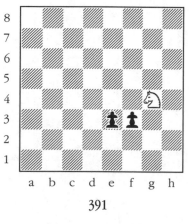

391

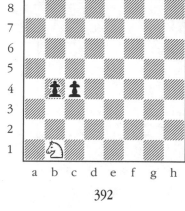

392

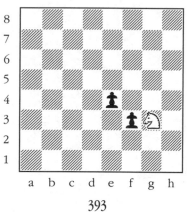

393

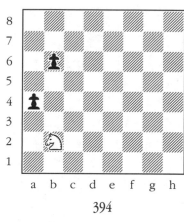

394

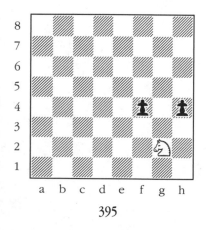

395

396

Pawns, Knights, Queens, Rooks, and Bishops

Queen against two pawns

White to move: Find the path to victory.

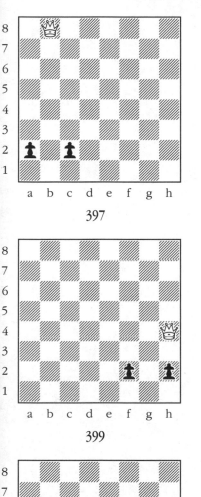

397

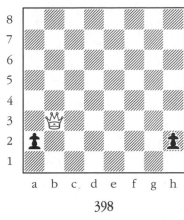

398

399

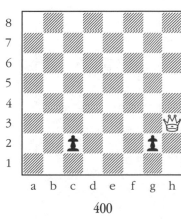

400

401

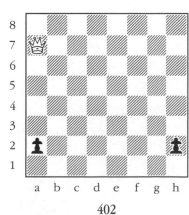

402

Pawns, Knights, Queens, Rooks, and Bishops

Queen against three pawns

Black to move: Find the path to victory.

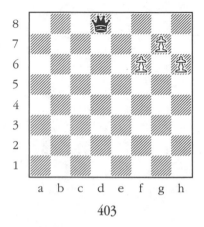

403

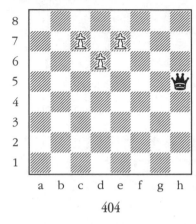

404

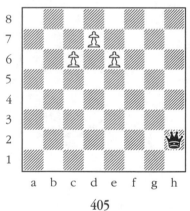

405

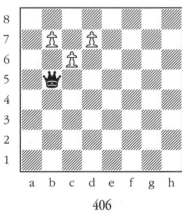

406

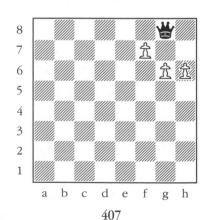

407

408

The King

Safe squares

White to move: Where can the white king go?
Find one or two possibilities.

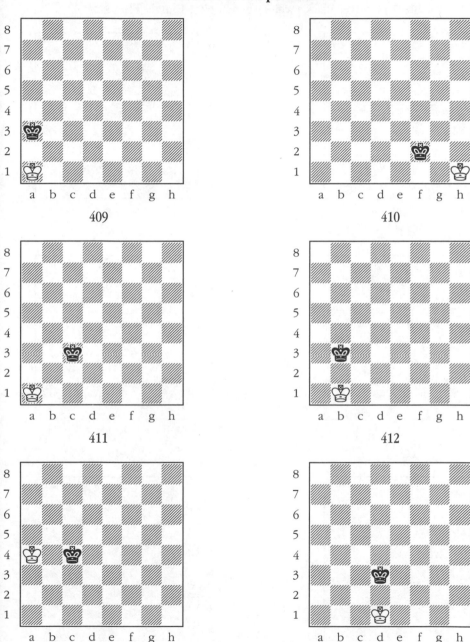

409

410

411

412

413

414

Kings, Pawns, Knights, Queens, Rooks, and Bishops

Attacking

Black to move: Attack a white pawn or piece with the black king.

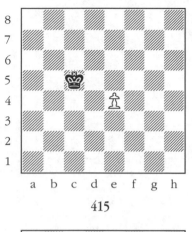

415

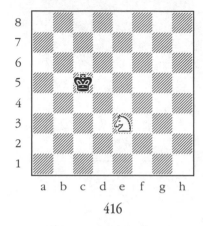

416

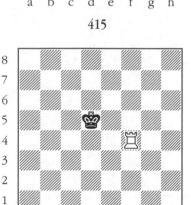

417

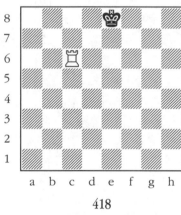

418

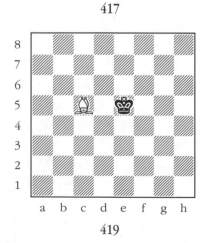

419

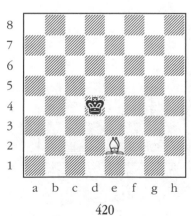

420

Kings, Pawns, Knights, Queens, Rooks, and Bishops

Double attack

White to move: Attack two black pieces or pawns with the king.

421

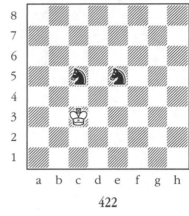

422

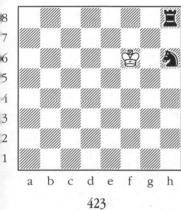

423

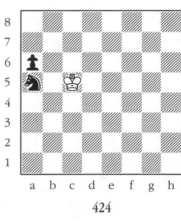

424

425

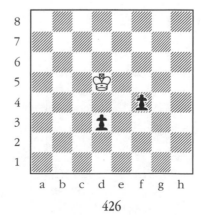

426

Kings, Pawns, Knights, Queens, Rooks, and Bishops

Capturing an undefended piece

Black to move: Which piece or pawn can be taken?

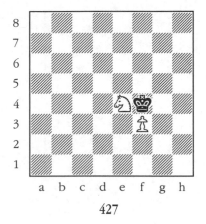

427

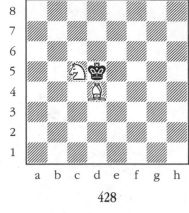

428

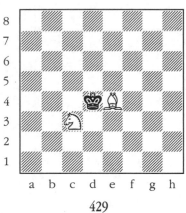

429

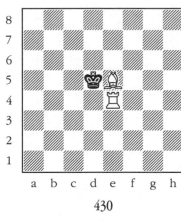

430

431

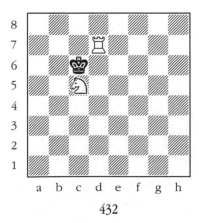

432

Kings, Pawns, Knights, Queens, Rooks, and Bishops

Escaping from a dungeon

White to move: Which piece or pawn can be taken?

433

434

435

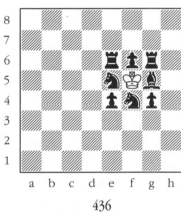

436

437

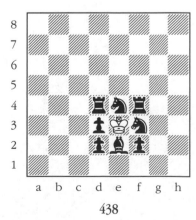

438

Kings, Pawns, Knights, Queens, Rooks, and Bishops

Defending

White to move: How to save a pawn or a piece?

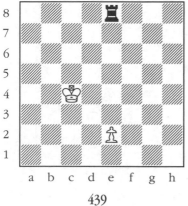

439

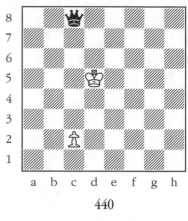

440

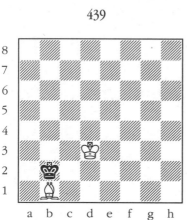

441

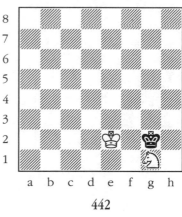

442

443

444

Kings, Pawns, Knights, Queens, Rooks, and Bishops
Defending
Black to move: How to save a pawn or a piece?

445

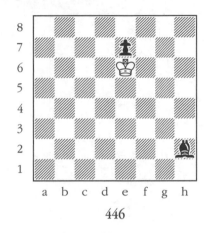

446

447

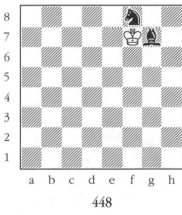

448

449

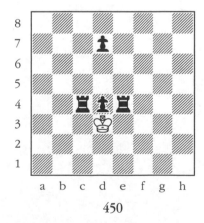

450

Kings, Pawns, Knights, Queens, Rooks, and Bishops

King against two pawns

White to move: Find the best move.

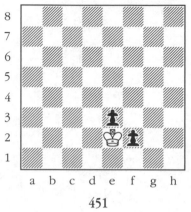

451

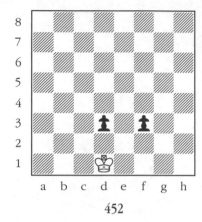

452

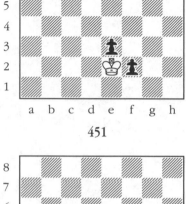

453

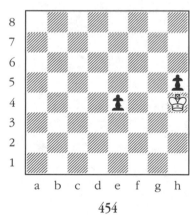

454

455

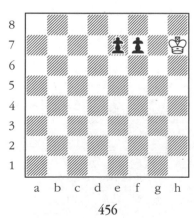

456

Kings, Pawns, Knights, Queens, Rooks, and Bishops

Trapping the rook

White to move: Catch the rook.

457

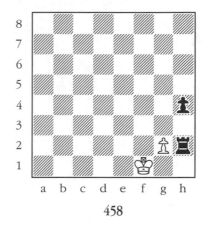

458

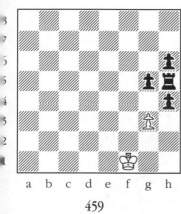

459

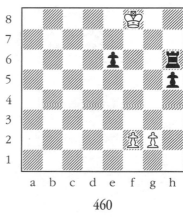

460

461

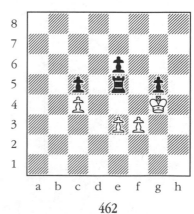

462

Kings, Pawns, Knights, Queens, Rooks, and Bishops

Trapping the bishop

Black to move: Catch the bishop.

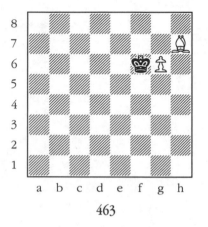

463

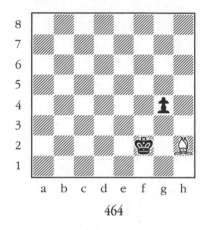

464

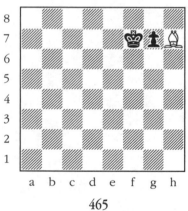

465

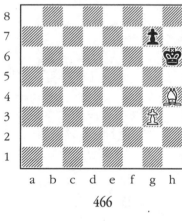

466

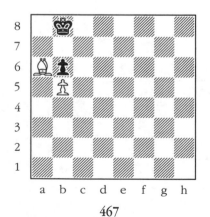

467

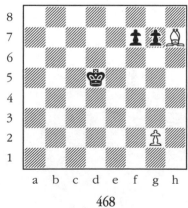

468

Kings, Pawns, Knights, Queens, Rooks, and Bishops

Trapping the queen

White to move: Catch the queen.

469

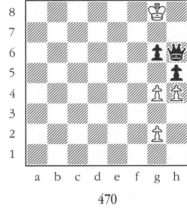

470

471

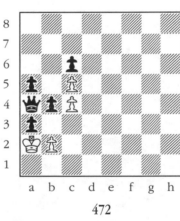

472

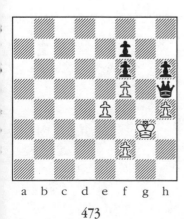

473

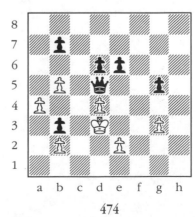

474

Kings, Pawns, Knights, Queens, Rooks, and Bishops

Trapping the knight

Black to move: Catch the knight.

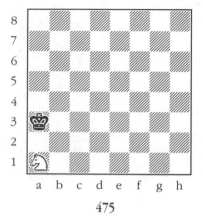

475

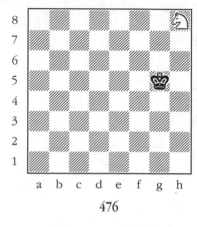

476

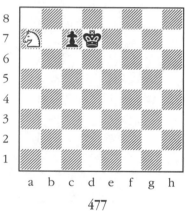

477

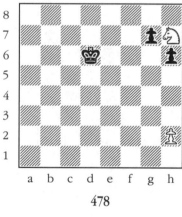

478

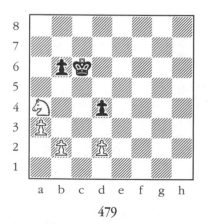

479

480

Kings, Pawns, Knights, Queens, Rooks, and Bishops

The pawn is desperate to become a queen

White to move: Find the best opportunity.

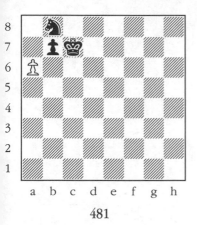

481

482

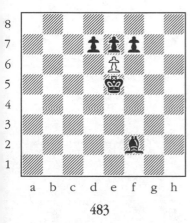

483

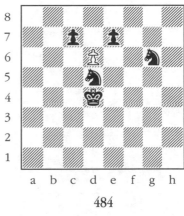

484

485

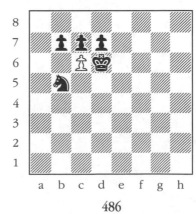

486

Check

Is it check or not?

White to move: Is the white king in check?

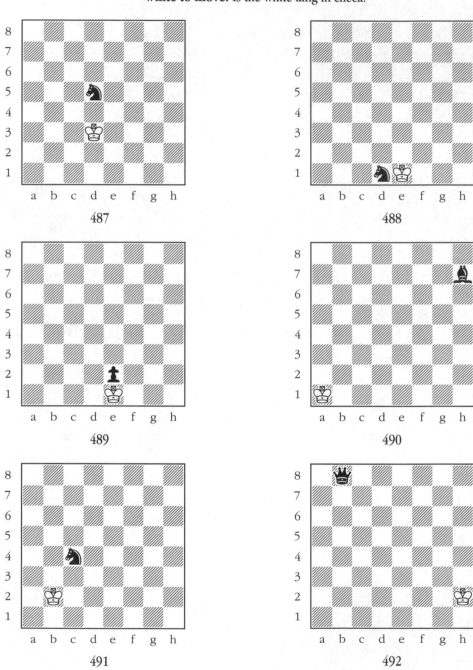

487

488

489

490

491

492

Check

Rook checks

White to move: Check with the rook in such a way that the king can't capture it.

493

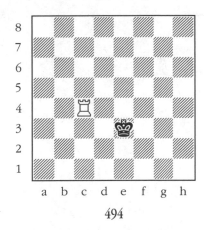

494

495

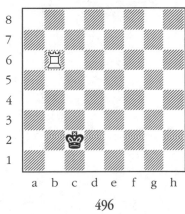

496

497

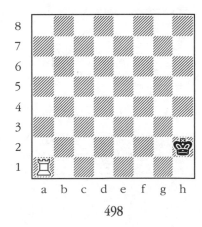

498

Check

Bishop checks

Black to move: Check with the bishop in such a way that the king can't take it.

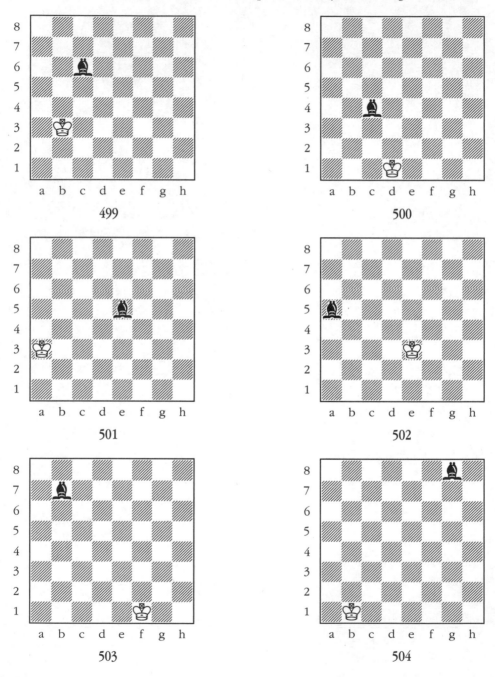

499

500

501

502

503

504

Check

Knight checks

White to move: Give check with the knight.

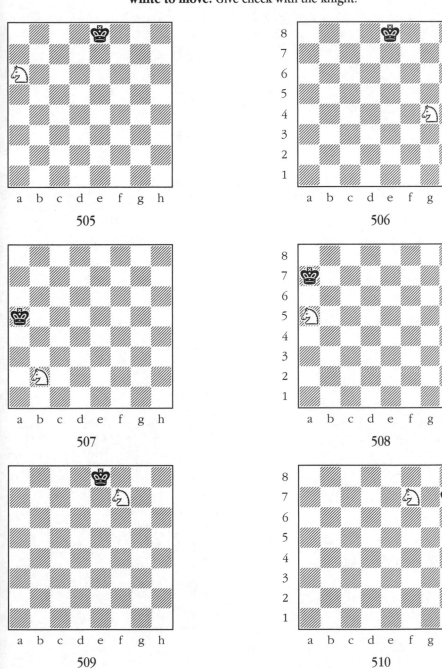

505

506

507

508

509

510

Check

Pawn checks

Black to move: Give check with a pawn move.

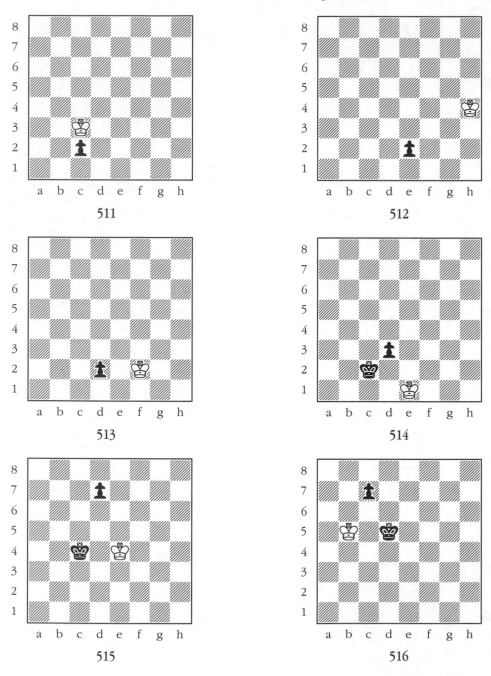

511

512

513

514

515

516

Check

Queen checks

White to move: Check with the queen in such a way that Black can't take it.

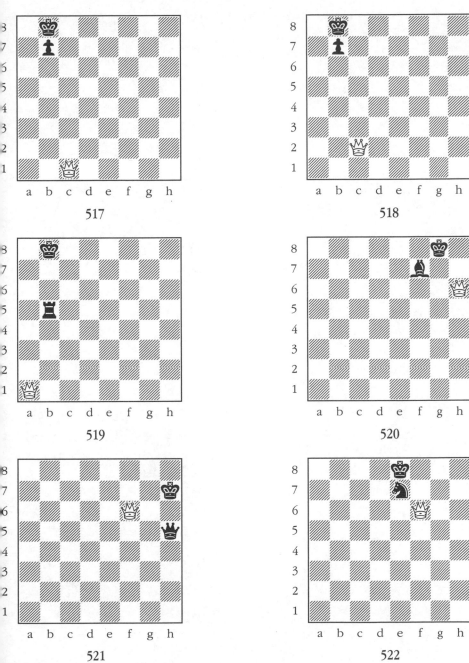

517

518

519

520

521

522

Check

Defending against check

Black to move: Find a defense.

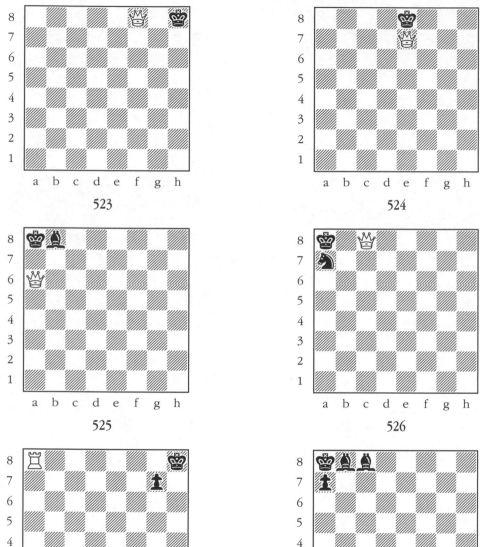

523

524

525

526

527

528

94

Check
Discovered check
White to move: Give a discovered check.

529

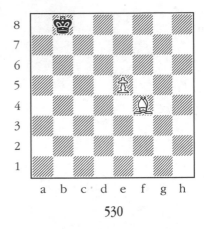

530

531

532

533

534

Check

Discovered check winning a piece

Black to move: Win a piece.

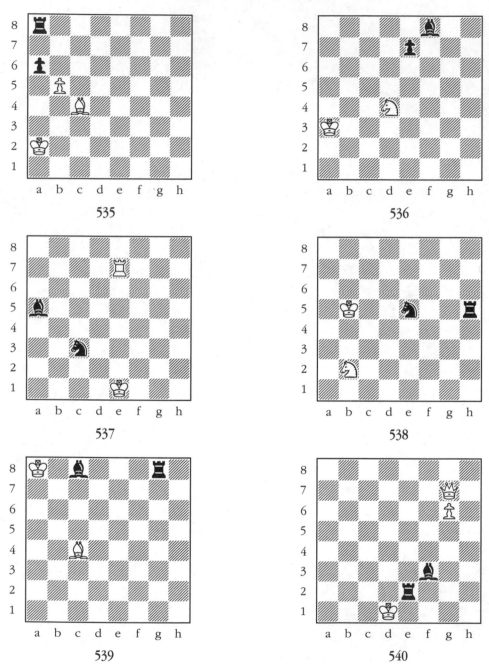

535

536

537

538

539

540

Check

Double check

White to move: Give double check.

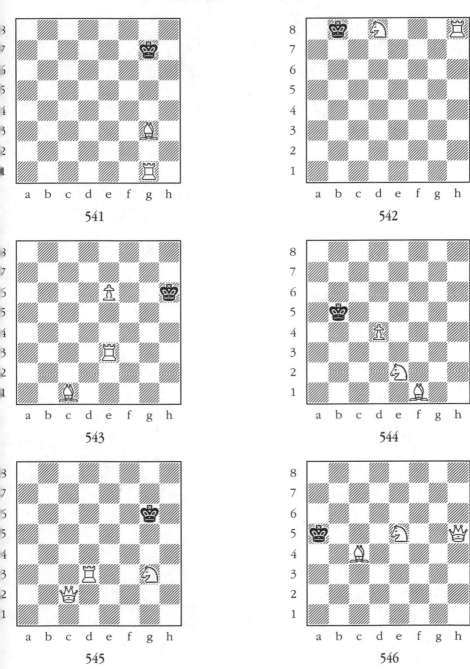

541

542

543

544

545

546

Check

Double check winning a piece

Black to move: Win a piece.

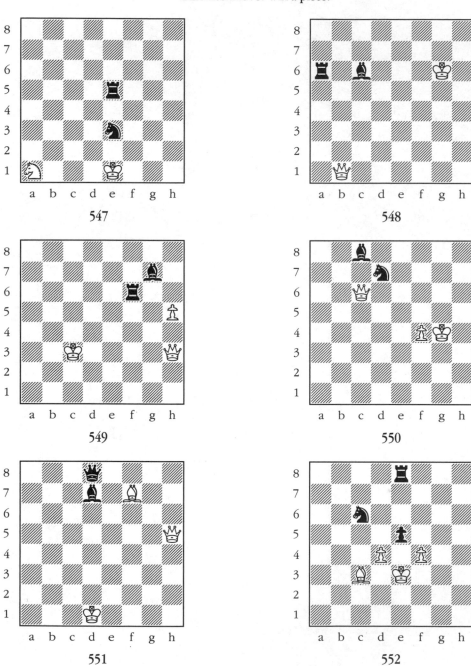

547

548

549

550

551

552

Checkmate

Is it checkmate or not?

Black to move: Has Black's king been checkmated?

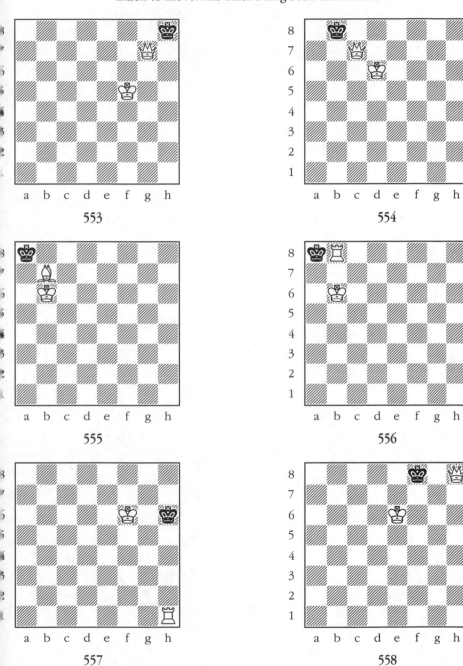

553

554

555

556

557

558

Checkmate

Is it checkmate or not?

White to move: Has White's king been checkmated?

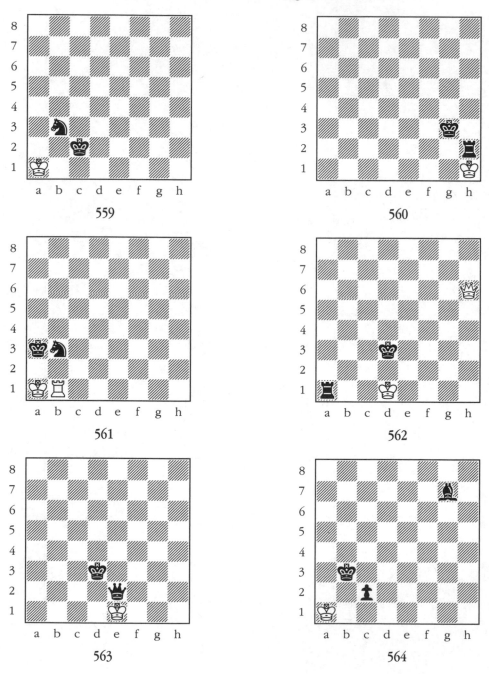

559

560

561

562

563

564

Stalemate

Is it stalemate or not?

Black to move: Is Black's king stalemated?

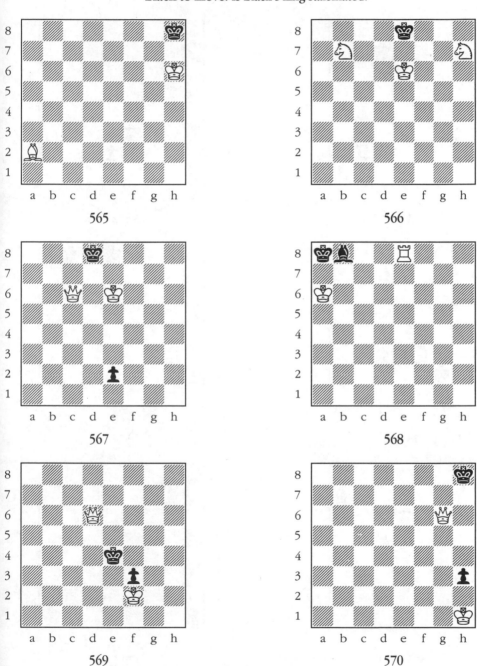

565

566

567

568

569

570

Stalemate

Is it stalemate or not?

White to move: Is White's king stalemated?

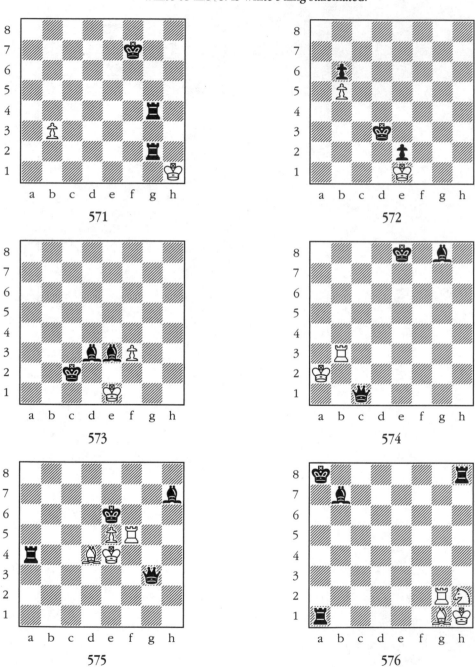

571

572

573

574

575

576

Checkmate and Stalemate
Is it checkmate or stalemate?
Black to move.

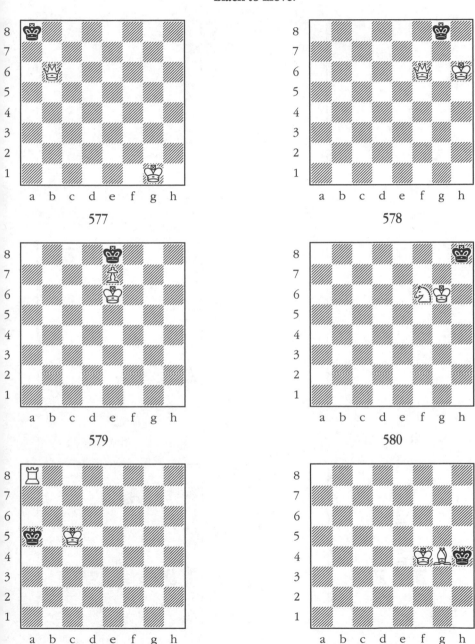

577

578

579

580

581

582

Checkmate and Stalemate

Is it checkmate or stalemate?

White to move.

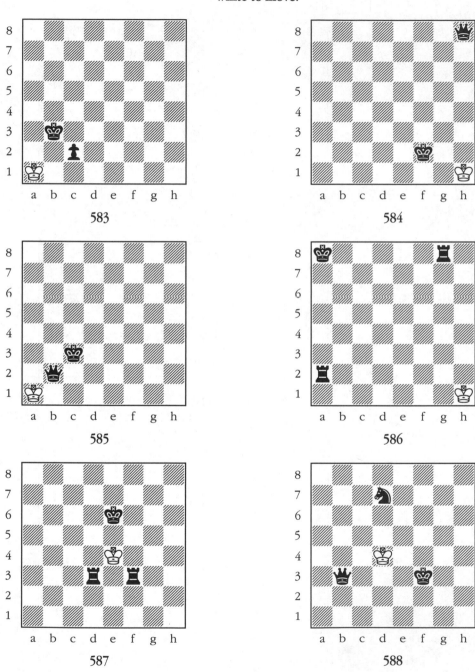

583

584

585

586

587

588

Perpetual Check

Perpetual check

White to move: Give perpetual check.

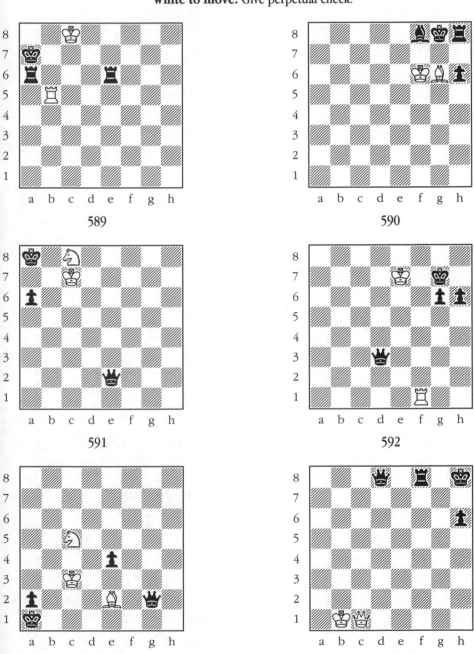

589

590

591

592

593

594

105

Perpetual Check

Perpetual check

Black to move: Give perpetual check.

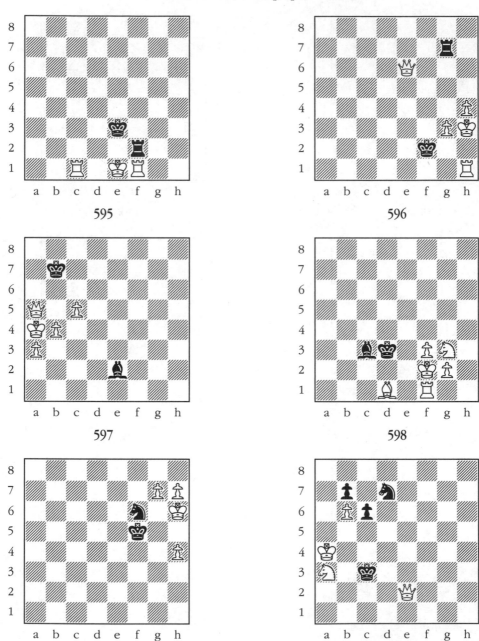

595

596

597

598

599

600

Castling

The rules for castling

White to move: Is castling allowed here?

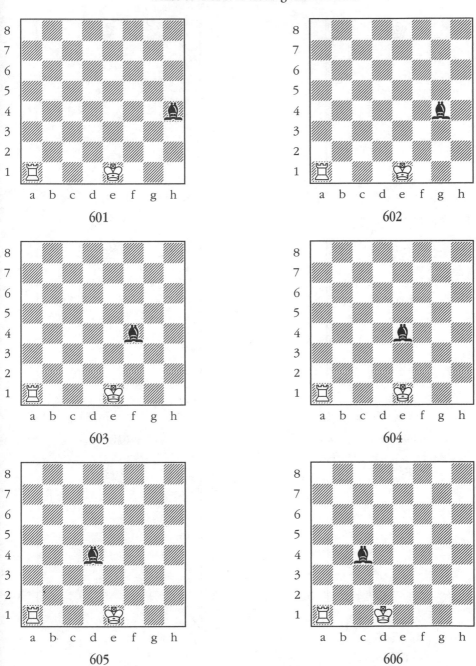

601

602

603

604

605

606

Castling

The rules for castling

Black to move: Is castling allowed here?

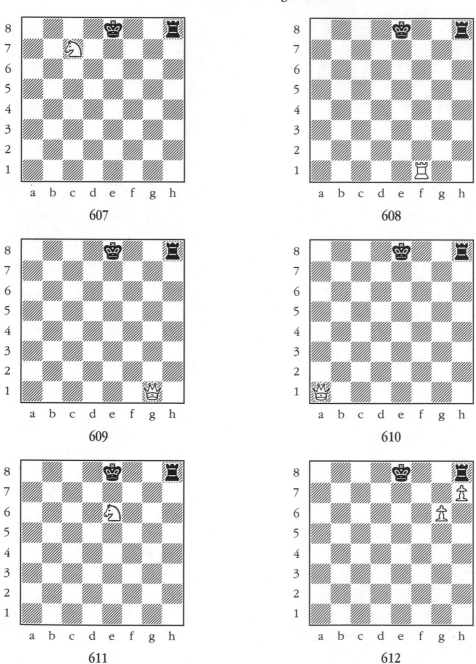

607

608

609

610

611

612

Capturing *en passant*
Captures

White to move: Black has just moved a pawn forward two squares.
Can it be taken *en passant?*

613

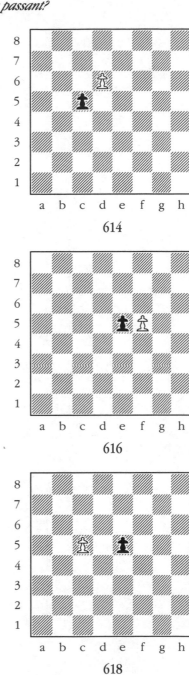

614

615

616

617

618

Capturing *en passant*

Captures

Black to move: White has just moved a pawn forward two squares.
Can it be taken *en passant?*

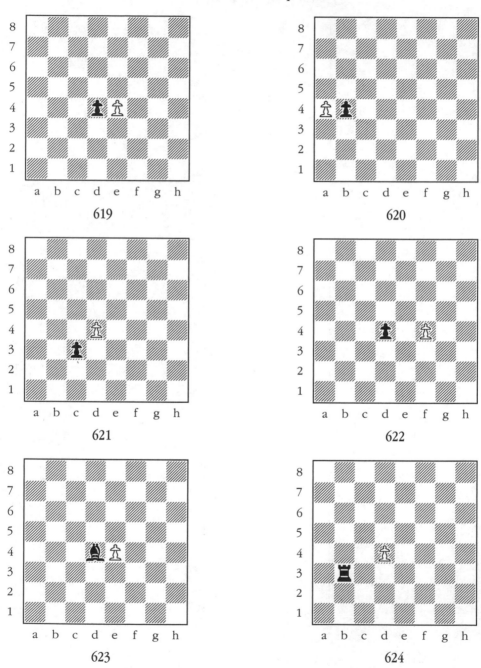

619

620

621

622

623

624

Solutions

1. Yes.
2. Yes.
3. Yes.
4. No.
5. No.
6. No.
7. 1... ♖xe1.
8. 1... ♖xg8.
9. 1... ♖xd3.
10. 1... ♖xa7.
11. 1... ♖xa7.
12. 1... ♖xa5.
13. No.
14. Yes.
15. Yes.
16. Yes.
17. Yes.
18. Yes.
19. 1... ♖xc8.
20. 1... ♖xh7.
21. 1... ♖xh8.
22. 1... ♖xc4.
23. 1... ♖xa8.
24. 1... ♖xh1.
25. Yes.
26. Yes.
27. No.
28. No.
29. Yes.
30. Yes.
31. 1... ♗xc3.
32. 1... ♗xh1.
33. 1... ♗xe1.
34. 1... ♗xd6.
35. 1... ♗xe5.
36. 1... ♗xb2.
37. ♗d4.
38. ♗b3.
39. ♗a1.
40. ♗a4.

41. ♗e1.
42. ♗h2.
43. 1. ♖d4, 1. ♖e5.
44. 1. ♖c7, 1. ♖e3.
45. 1. ♖b8, 1. ♖e3.
46. 1. ♖b7, 1. ♖f5.
47. 1. ♖a2, 1. ♖h3.
48. 1. ♖a8, 1. ♖h1.
49. 1... ♗b7.
50. 1... ♗f4.
51. 1... ♗e6.
52. 1... ♗e4.
53. 1... ♗f4.
54. 1... ♗b7.
55. 1. ♖e5.
56. 1. ♖h2.
57. 1. ♖e8.
58. 1. ♖d5.
59. 1. ♖a2.
60. 1. ♖c2.
61. 1... ♗e5.
62. 1... ♗d2.
63. 1... ♗c6.
64. 1... ♗c5.
65. 1... ♗c4.
66. 1... ♗d5.
67. 1. ♖a8.
68. 1. ♖h8.
69. 1. ♖a8.
70. 1. ♖h7.
71. 1. ♖a4.
72. 1. ♖f1.
73. 1... ♗g7.
74. 1... ♗e4.
75. 1... ♗d8.
76. 1... ♗f7.
77. 1... ♗f1.
78. 1... ♗a7.
79. 1. ♖xh1.
80. 1. ♗xd3.

81. 1. ♖xh1.
82. 1. ♗xh2.
83. 1. ♖xd8.
84. 1. ♖xh4.
85. 1. ♖a8 (now one of the black pieces is forced to make a move, leaving the other piece under attack; for example: 1... ♖h4 2. ♖xg8).
86. 1. ♖e6.
87. 1. ♖aa5 (but not 1. ♖f2 because of 1... ♗g4 or 1... ♗g6).
88. 1. ♖h2.
89. 1. ♖ae2.
90. 1. ♖b5.
91. 1... ♖a8, and then, for example: 2. ♖a5 ♗b7.
92. 1... ♗g7.
93. 1... ♗b7.
94. 1... ♖g7.
95. 1... ♗b8 (an attack in reply).
96. 1... ♖e3 2. ♗xd2 ♖d3 (winning back the piece).
97. 1. ♖b1.
98. 1. ♖h4.
99. 1. ♖c8.
100. 1. ♖e2.
101. 1. ♗d5.
102. 1. ♖d4.
103. 1... ♗g2.
104. 1... ♗a7.
105. 1... ♗f5.
106. 1... ♗e3.
107. 1... ♖f1.
108. 1... ♗b2.
109. 1. ♖xa3 (but not 1. ♖xc5 ♗xc5 2. ♖xa7 ♗xa7).

110. 1. ♖xc5.
111. 1. ♖xa5.
112. 1. ♖xg8.
113. 1. ♖xa8.
114. 1. ♖h2 ♖xh2 2. ♗xf3.
115. Yes.
116. Yes.
117. Yes.
118. No.
119. No.
120. No.
121. 1... ♕f1.
122. 1... ♕a7.
123. 1... ♕c7.
124. 1... ♕f5.
125. 1... ♕f8.
126. 1... ♕c3.
127. 1. ♕b8, 1. ♕c1, 1. ♕c2.
128. 1. ♕a4, 1. ♕b4, 1. ♕h3.
129. 1. ♕c7, 1. ♕h1, 1. ♕h6.
130. 1. ♕b3, 1. ♕d7, 1. ♕h7.
131. 1. ♕e3, 1. ♕f7, 1. ♕f8.
132. 1. ♕b8, 1. ♕f8, 1. ♕g4.
133. 1. ♕f6.
134. 1. ♕h3.
135. 1. ♕c2.
136. 1. ♕b3.
137. 1. ♕g1.
138. 1. ♕b8.
139. 1... ♕b1.
140. 1... ♕f3.
141. 1... ♕e5.
142. 1... ♕e2.
143. 1... ♕c3.
144. 1... ♕d1.

145. 1. ♗d4.

146. 1. ♖a8.

147. 1. ♖e1.

148. 1. ♖g1.

149. 1. ♖b4.

150. 1. ♖a2.

151. 1...♕xh7.

152. 1...♕xh8.

153. 1...♕xh4.

154. 1...♕xe5.

155. 1...♕xb4.

156. 1...♕xd3.

157. 1. ♔h1 (and Black loses a piece because of the pin).

158. 1. ♕c8.

159. 1. ♗f3.

160. 1. ♗b2.

161. 1. ♕g5.

162. 1. ♔h5.

163. 1...♕b2.

164. 1...♕g2.

165. 1...♗h2.

166. 1...♖d3.

167. 1...♕c3.

168. 1...♖f1.

169. 1. ♔b1.

170. 1. ♗g2.

171. 1. ♗e7.

172. 1. ♕d5.

173. 1. ♖c2.

174. 1. ♖b3.

175. No.

176. No.

177. No.

178. Yes.

179. Yes.

180. Yes.

181. 1...♘xd3.

182. 1...♘xc4.

183. 1...♘xg3.

184. 1...♘xf7.

185. 1...♘xe3.

186. 1...♘xf4.

187. 1...♘g6.

188. 1...♘c7.

189. 1...♘a6.

190. 1...♘f6.

191. 1...♘g5.

192. 1...♘c6.

193. No.

194. No.

195. No.

196. Yes.

197. Yes.

198. Yes.

199. 1...♘d4.

200. 1...♘e4.

201. 1...♘e5.

202. 1...♘xd4.

203. 1...♘c5.

204. 1...♘e4.

205. 1. ♖b7.

206. 1. ♖f6.

207. 1. ♖d6.

208. 1. ♖e6.

209. 1. ♖d5.

210. 1. ♖e5.

211. 1. ♗h5.

212. 1. ♗d8.

213. 1. ♗b5.

214. 1. ♗g5.

215. 1. ♗d6.

216. 1. ♗e5.

217. 1...♕d1.

218. 1...♕g2.

219. 1...♕d3.

220. 1...♕d4.

221. 1...♕f3.

222. 1...♕c4.

223. 1. ♘c7.

224. 1. ♘f6.

225. 1. ♘d6.

226. 1. ♘e7.

227. 1. ♘f5.

228. 1. ♘c4.

229. 1...♘f2.

230. 1...♘c5.

231. 1...♘c2.

232. 1...♘f3.

233. 1...♘e6.

234. 1...♘f5.

235. 1. ♘xc2.

236. 1. ♘xe2.

237. 1. ♘xb2.

238. 1. ♘xf5.

239. 1. ♘xd2.

240. 1. ♘xd2.

241. 1...♖e8.

242. 1...♘a6.

243. 1...♗d5.

244. 1...♖g8.

245. 1...♗f1.

246. 1...♕h8.

247. 1. ♖c8.

248. 1. ♖a8.

249. 1. ♘f7.

250. 1. ♖e8.

251. 1. ♗d4.

252. 1. ♕e1.

253. 1...♗b7.

254. 1...♘e6.

255. 1...♖b8.

256. 1...♖h3.

257. 1...♘f2.

258. 1...♘xf5.

259. No.

260. No.

261. No.

262. No.

263. Yes.

264. Yes.

265. 1...h3.

266. 1...dxe4.

267. 1...g3.

268. 1...h6.

269. 1...d3.

270. 1...g4.

271. 1. cxb4.

272. 1. exf5.

273. 1. dxe5.

274. 1. exd5.

275. 1. cxd5.

276. 1. dxc5.

277. No.

278. No.

279. Yes.

280. Yes.

281. Yes.

282. Yes.

283. 1. bxa6.

284. 1. fxg6.

285. 1. exf4.

286. 1. dxc5.

287. 1. exd5.

288. 1. gxh4.

289. 1...a5.

290. 1...f5.

291. 1...e5.

292. 1...c5.

293. 1...c5.

294. 1...c5.

295. 1. e4.

296. 1. d4.

297. 1. e4.

298. 1. exd4.

299. 1. e5.

300. 1. a5.

301. 1...a1♕, 1...a1♖.

302. 1...e1♕, 1...e1♗.

303. 1...f1♕, 1...f1♖.

304. 1...f1♕, 1...f1♗.

305. 1...h1♘.

306. 1...d1♘.

307. 1...c3 2. dxc3 e3, and the black pawn queens first.

308. 1...c3 2. dxc3 dxe3.

309. 1...g4 2. hxg4 h3.

310. 1...b3 2. cxb3 d3.

311. 1...b3 2. axb3 axb3.

312. 1...f3 2. exf3 (2. gxf3 e3 3. fxe3 g3) 2...g3 3. fxg3 e3.

313. 1. b5.

314. 1. g5 fxg5 2. f6.

315. 1. c6 dxc6 3. dxe6.

316. 1. e5 dxe5 2. d6 exd6 3. f6.

317. 1. b6 cxb6 2. d6.

318. 1. d5 cxd5 2. b5.

319. 1. a4.

320. 1. e3.

321. 1. h3.

322. 1. c4.

323. 1. f3.

324. 1. c4.

325. 1...e5.

326. 1...g6.

327. 1...b5.

328. 1...e4.

329. 1...e5.

330. 1...c5.

331. 1. cxd7.

332. 1. gxf7.

333. 1. dxc6.

334. 1. exd5.

335. 1. cxd4.

336. 1. gxf6.

337. 1...g5.

338. 1...e5.

339. 1...d5.

340. 1...f6.

341. 1...e5.

342. 1...a3.

343. 1. ♖h2.

344. 1. ♕g1.

345. 1. ♗f3.

346. 1. ♘d5.

347. 1. ♘e3.

348. 1. ♕a2.

349. 1...♗b7.

350. 1...♘f7.

351. 1...e4.

352. 1...♘g3.

353. 1... ♖e8.

354. 1...♘e3.

355. 1. ♖a3.

356. 1. ♖f8.

357. 1. ♗g7.

358. 1. ♗c7.

359. 1. ♘f2.

360. 1. ♘c3.

361. 1. ♖xh2.

362. 1. ♖d3.

363. 1. ♖d4.

364. 1. ♖d1.

365. 1. ♖e1.

366. 1. ♖c8.

367. 1...a2.

368. 1...c2.

369. 1...e2. 2. ♖a1 d3.

370. 1...e2 2. ♖xd2 e1♕.

371. 1...d2 2. ♖d6 e3.

372. 1...f4. 2. ♖d1 e2.

373. 1. ♗g3.

374. 1. ♗f3.

375. 1. ♗c1 e2 2. ♗d2.

376. 1. ♗h1 f2 2. ♗g2.

377. 1. ♗f6 (1...f5 was threatened).

378. 1. ♗c8 h2 2. ♗b7.

379. 1...e2.

380. 1...f2.

381. 1...h3.

382. 1...d3 2. ♗b4 a2.

383. 1...g3 2. ♗e6 g2.

384. 1...f3.

385. 1. ♘e2.

386. 1. ♘e2.

387. 1. ♘xa2.

388. 1. ♘g5.

389. 1. ♘h3.

390. 1. ♘h3 (but not 1. ♘xg2 h3).

391. 1...e2.

392. 1...c3.

393. 1...e3.

394. 1...a3.

395. 1...h3.

396. 1...d3.

397. 1. ♕b2.

398. 1. ♕d1.

399. 1. ♕h3.

400. 1. ♕e3.

401. 1. ♕c5.

402. 1. ♕a8.

403. 1...♕g8.

404. 1...♕e8.

405. 1...♕d6.

406. 1...♕b6.

407. 1...♕f8.

408. 1...♕c2 2. a7 ♕c6.

409. 1. ♔b1.

410. 1. ♔h2.

411. 1. ♔a2, 1. ♔b1.

412. 1. ♔a1, 1. ♔c1.

413. 1. ♔a3, 1. ♔a5.

414. 1. ♔c1, 1. ♔e1.

415. 1...♔d4.

416. 1...♔d4.

417. 1...♔e5.

418. 1...♔d7.

419. 1...♔d5.

420. 1...♔e3.

421. 1. ♔g2.

422. 1. ♔d4.

423. 1. ♔g7.

424. 1. ♔b6.

425. 1. ♔d7.

426. 1. ♔e4.

427. 1...♔xf3.

428. 1...♔xd4.

429. 1...♔xc3.

430. 1...♔xe4.

431. 1...♔xf5.

432. 1...♔xc5.

433. 1. ♔xa5.

434. 1. ♔xe3.

435. 1. ♔xd3.

436. 1. ♔xe4.

437. 1. ♔xd3.

438. 1. ♔xf4.

439. 1. ♔d3.

440. 1. c4.

441. 1. ♗c2.

442. 1. ♘f3.

443. 1. ♘g3.

444. 1. ♗c4.

445. 1...♔f3.

446. 1...♗d6.

447. 1...♘f6.

448. 1...♗h6.

449. 1...♗d5.

450. 1...d5.

451. 1. ♔f1.

452. 1. ♔e1.

453. 1. ♔a2.

454. 1. ♔g3.

455. 1. ♔a6 c5 2. ♔b5.

456. 1. ♔h6 e5 2. ♔g5 (or 2. ♔h5).

457. 1. ♔b1.

458. 1. ♔g1.

459. 1. g4.

460. 1. ♔g7.

461. 1. a4.

462. 1. e4.

463. 1...♔g7.

464. 1...g3.

465. 1...g6.

466. 1...g5.

467. 1...♔c7.

468. 1...g6 2. ♗g8 ♔e6.

469. 1. ♔b1.

470. 1. g5.

471. 1. ♔f7.

472. 1. b3.

473. 1. f3.

474. 1. e4.
475. 1...♔b2.
476. 1...♔f6.
477. 1...c6.
478. 1...♔e7.
479. 1...b5.
480. 1...g5.
481. 1. a7.
482. 1. f7.
483. 1. exf7.
484. 1. d7.
485. 1. b7.
486. 1. cxb7.
487. No.
488. No.
489. No.
490. No.
491. Yes.
492. Yes.
493. 1. ♖d4+.
494. 1. ♖c3+.
495. 1. ♖g2+.
496. 1. ♖c6+.
497. 1. ♖b1+.
498. 1. ♖a2+.
499. 1...♗d5+.
500. 1...♗b3+.
501. 1...♗d6+.
502. 1...♗b6+.
503. 1...♗a6+.
504. 1...♗h7+.
505. 1. ♘c7+.
506. 1. ♘f6+.
507. 1. ♘c4+.
508. 1. ♘c6+.
509. 1. ♘d6+.
510. 1. ♘g5+.
511. 1...c1♕+, 1...c1♖+.
512. 1...e1♕+, 1...e1♗+.
513. 1...d1♘+.

514. 1...d2+.
515. 1...d5+.
516. 1...c6+.
517. 1. ♕f4+.
518. 1. ♕h2+.
519. 1. ♕h8+.
520. 1. ♕g5+.
521. 1. ♕e7+.
522. 1. ♕h8+.
523. 1...♔h7.
524. 1...♔xe7.
525. 1...♗a7.
526. 1...♘xc8.
527. 1...♔h7.
528. 1...♗b7.
529. 1. e5+.
530. 1. e6+.
531. 1. fxe6+.
532. 1. ♔h2+.
533. 1. ♘f1+.
534. 1. ♘d3+.
535. 1...axb5+.
536. 1...e5+.
537. 1...♘d5+.
538. 1...♘d3+.
539. 1...♗e6+.
540. 1...♖e7+.
541. 1. ♗e5++.
542. 1. ♘c6++.
543. 1. ♖h3++.
544. 1. ♘c3++.
545. 1. ♖d6++.
546. 1. ♘c6++.
547. 1...♘c2++.
548. 1...♗e4++.
549. 1...♖f3++.
550. 1...♘e5++.
551. 1...♗g4++.
552. 1...exd4++.
553. No.
554. No.
555. No.

556. No.
557. Yes.
558. Yes.
559. No.
560. No.
561. No.
562. No.
563. Yes.
564. Yes.
565. Stalemate.
566. Stalemate.
567. Not stalemate.
568. Stalemate.
569. Not stalemate.
570. Not stalemate.
571. Not stalemate.
572. Not stalemate.
573. Not stalemate.
574. Stalemate.
575. Stalemate.
576. Stalemate.
577. Stalemate.
578. Stalemate.
579. Stalemate.
580. Stalemate.
581. Checkmate.
582. Stalemate.
583. Stalemate.
584. Checkmate.
585. Checkmate.
586. Stalemate.
587. Stalemate.
588. Stalemate.
589. 1. ♖b7+ ♔a8 2. ♖b8+ ♔a7.
590. 1. ♗f7+ ♔h7 2. ♗g6+ ♔g8.
591. 1. ♘b6+ ♔a7 2. ♘c8+ ♔a8.
592. 1. ♖f7+ ♔g8 (or 1...♔h8) 2. ♖f8+ ♔g7 (or 1...♔h7).

593. 1. ♘b3+ ♔b1 2. ♘d2+ ♔a1 (or 2...♔c1) 3. ♘b3+.
594. 1. ♕xh6+ ♔g8 2. ♕g6+ ♔h8.
595. 1...♖e2+ 2. ♔d1 ♖d2+.
596. 1...♖xg3+ 2. ♔h2 ♖g2+.
597. 1...♗d1+ 2. ♔b5 ♗e2+.
598. 1...♗d4+ 2. ♔e1 ♗c3+.
599. 1...♘g4+ 2. ♔h5 ♘f6+.
600. 1...♘c5+ 2. ♔a5 ♘b3+.
601. No.
602. No.
603. No.
604. Yes.
605. Yes.
606. No.
607. No.
608. No.
609. No.
610. Yes.
611. No.
612. No.
613. Yes.
614. No.
615. No.
616. Yes.
617. No.
618. No.
619. Yes.
620. Yes.
621. No.
622. No.
623. No.
624. No.